Discour

D0260539

Discourse analysis does not attempt to reveal psychological universals but rather is concerned with the social context in which subjects' responses are generated. Instead of studying the mind as if it were outside language, psychologists using discourse analysis study the spoken and written texts where images of the mind are reproduced and transformed.

Discourse Analytic Research is designed to meet the growing need among undergraduate and postgraduate psychology students for clear illustrations of discourse analytic work, and to provide an empirically demonstrable critique of traditional psychological approaches.

In illustrating the variety of methods available through their studies of punk identity, sexual jealousy, images of nature, political talk, sexism in radio, education case conferences and occupational choice, the contributors provide a fascinating and challenging presentation of discourse analysis for all psychologists.

Erica Burman is Senior Lecturer in Developmental and Educational Psychology, and **Ian Parker** is Senior Lecturer in Social and Abnormal Psychology, both at the Manchester Metropolitan University. Ian Parker is the author of *Discourse Dynamics* and Erica Burman is the author of *Deconstructing Developmental Psychology*, both published by Routledge.

Also available from Routledge:

Discourse Dynamics
Critical Analysis for Social and Individual Psychology
Ian Parker

Deconstructing Social Psychology
Edited by Ian Parker and John Shotter

The Crisis in Modern Social Psychology
And How to End it
Ian Parker

Significant Differences
Feminism in Psychology
Corinne Squire

Mastery of Reason
Cognitive Development and the Production of Rationality
Valerie Walkerdine

Decoding Development Psychology
Erica Burman

Discourse analytic research

Repertoires and readings of texts in action

Edited by Erica Burman
and Ian Parker

London and New York

First published 1993
by Routledge
11 New Fetter Lane, London EC4P 4EE

Simultaneously published in the USA and Canada
by Routledge
29 West 35th Street, New York, NY 10001

© 1993 Selection and editorial matter, Erica Burman and Ian Parker;
individual chapters, the contributors

Phototypeset in Bembo by
Mews Photosetting, Beckenham, Kent
Printed and bound in Great Britain by
Biddles Ltd, Guildford and King's Lynn

British Library Cataloguing in Publication Data
A catalogue record for this book is available from the British Library

Library of Congress Cataloging in Publication Data
Discourse analytic research: repertoires and readings of texts in
action / edited by Erica Burman and Ian Parker.
p.   cm.
Includes bibliographical references and index.
1. Discourse analysis – Psychological aspects. I. Burman, Erica.
II. Parker, Ian. 1956–
P302.8.D57   1993
401'.41–dc20   92-47441
                                                                    CIP

ISBN 0-415-09720-7
      0-415-09721-5 (pbk)

Contents

Part III Discourse, action and the research process

Contributors

Erica Burman is a Senior Lecturer in Developmental and Educational Psychology at the Manchester Metropolitan University Discourse Unit, Department of Psychology and Speech Pathology, Gaskell Campus, Hathersage Road, Manchester, M13 0JA.

Rosalind Gill is a Lecturer at Brunel University of West London, Department of Human Sciences, Uxbridge, Middlesex, UB8 3PH.

Deborah Marks is Susan Isaacs Research Fellow and a Lecturer at the Manchester Metropolitan University Discourse Unit, Department of Psychology and Speech Pathology, Gaskell Campus, Hathersage Road, Manchester, M13 0JA.

Harriette Marshall is a Lecturer in Social Psychology at the University of East London, Department of Psychology, Romford Road, London, E15 4LZ.

Philip Macnaghten is a Researcher at the Centre for Environmental Change, Fylde College, University of Lancaster, Bailrigg, Lancaster, LA1 4YN.

James Moir is a Lecturer in the Department of Business Studies, Dundee Institute of Technology, Bell Street, Dundee, DD1 1HG.

Ian Parker is a Senior Lecturer in Social and Abnormal Psychology at the Manchester Metropolitan University Discourse Unit, Department of Psychology and Speech Pathology, Gaskell Campus, Hathersage Road, Manchester, M13 0JA.

Bianca Raabe is a Research Student at the University of East London, Department of Psychology, Romford Road, London, E15 4LZ.

Paul Stenner is a Lecturer in Social Psychology at the University of East London, Department of Psychology, Romford Road, London, E15 4LZ.

Sue Widdicombe is a Lecturer in Social Psychology at the University of Edinburgh, 7 George Square, Edinburgh, Scotland, EH8 9JZ.

Chapter 1

Introduction – discourse analysis: the turn to the text

Erica Burman and Ian Parker

This book is part of a new wave of research sweeping across social psychology, and breaking down boundaries between social psychology and other parts of the discipline. The chapters collected here illustrate the way that discourse analysis can help us reformulate what it is that developmental and social psychologists, personality theorists and cognitive scientists think they are doing when they try to study what goes on 'inside' the individual. We argue that personality profiles for different jobs (Moir, Chapter 2, this volume), attitudes towards social issues (Marshall and Raabe, Chapter 3, this volume; Macnaghten, Chapter 4, this volume), prejudice towards women (Gill, Chapter 5, this volume), personal identity (Widdicombe, Chapter 6, this volume) and even deeply felt emotions like jealousy (Stenner, Chapter 7, this volume) are not things hiding inside the person which a psychologist can then 'discover' but are created by the language that is used to describe them. Psychological phenomena have a public and collective reality, and we are mistaken if we think that they have their origin in the private space of the individual.

Language organized into *discourses* (what some contributors here call ~~interpretative repertoires~~) has an immense power to shape the way that people, ~~including psychologists~~, experience and behave in the world. Language contains the most basic categories that we use to understand ourselves; affecting the way we act as women or as men (in, for example, the sets of arguments that are given about the nature of gender difference deployed to justify inequality), and reproducing the way we define our cultural identity (in, for example, the problems and solutions we negotiate when we try and define who we are as a member of a minority group). When we talk about any phenomenon (our personality, attitudes, emotions), we draw on shared meanings (so we know that the listener will know what we are saying). Many discourse analysts in psychology now would say that we draw on shared patterns of meaning and contrasting ways of speaking they would call repertoires (Potter and Wetherell, 1987) or discourses (Hollway, 1989; Parker, 1992) or ideological dilemmas (Billig *et al.*, 1988). Instead of studying the mind as if it were outside language, we study the spoken and written texts (and other types of text) − the conversations, debates, discussions where images of the mind are reproduced and transformed.

The traditional methods used by psychology are not going to get us very far in identifying the semantic processes going on in language as people recreate the phenomena psychologists usually want to understand (and measure). The 'experimental discourse' (a set of statements, terms, metaphors and turns of phrase which include 'subjects', 'control conditions', 'variables' and 'results') is quite inappropriate here. Our problem now, a series of dilemmas we have to negotiate in the course of this book, is how to develop alternative methods as part of discourse analytic work. Although there have been attempts to set out 'how to do' discourse analysis (Potter and Wetherell, 1987; Fairclough, 1989; Parker, 1992), there is a danger of pretending that there is a simple method for gathering discourses (as if they could appear like the rest of the data psychologists collect) and of glossing over the differences between discourse analysts. Some contributors in this book are happy to talk about 'repertoires' (Moir, Chapter 2; Marshall and Raabe, Chapter 3), 'discourses' (Macnaghten, Chapter 4; Marks, Chapter 8) or 'practical ideologies' (Gill, Chapter 5), while others prefer to avoid reifying these meanings (treating them as if they were 'things') and talk about focusing on 'dynamic and pragmatic aspects of language use' (Widdicombe, Chapter 6) or a 'thematic decomposition' which identifies 'subject positions' (Stenner, Chapter 7).

This refocusing of research in psychology, both in terms of the substantive issues we can address, and in terms of the variety of methods we could use, is the most important and complex contribution of discourse analysis to the discipline. In the rest of this chapter we want to outline key reference points for the development of discourse analysis, explore further how the turn to the text is useful for those who wish to transform rather than simply reproduce psychology, and then briefly raise some questions about the nature of this research, issues that will be picked up in Chapter 9.

REFERENCE POINTS IN THE DEVELOPMENT OF DISCOURSE ANALYTIC RESEARCH

The variety of debates in discourse research can be bewildering for a researcher new to the area who may simply be out to pick up a useful set of analytic and theoretical tools. In part this is due to the proliferation of brands of discourse analysis and their multiple origins, each of which involve different emphases or levels and styles of analysis. Indeed, it is very difficult to speak of 'discourse' or even 'discourse analysis' as a single unitary entity, since this would blur together approaches subscribing to specific and different philosophical frameworks. In so far as there could be said to be commonality, these approaches are united by a common attention to the significance and structuring effects of language, and are associated with interpretive and reflexive styles of analysis.

What the different theoretical models used by the contributors to this book share is a concern with the ways language produces and constrains meaning, where meaning does not, or does not only, reside within individuals' heads, and where social conditions give rise to the forms of talk available. In its various forms, discourse analysis offers a social account of subjectivity by attending to the linguistic resources by which the sociopolitical realm is produced and reproduced. Such a characterization places discourse analysis as the latest successor to, or version of, approaches such as hermeneutics (Gauld and Shotter, 1977) and social semiotics (Hodge and Kress, 1988). All involve an attention to the ways in which language (as with other representational systems) does more than reflect what it represents, with the corresponding implication that meanings are multiple and shifting, rather than unitary and fixed. Not only is the relationship between what is 'inside' and 'outside' language problematized by these approaches, but the very terms and tools of our inquiry and evaluation become matters of interpretation and debate.

It is possible to identify three reference points in discourse analytic research in psychology now. These reference points are not coherent, unitary theoretical positions or types of method. They are, rather, the clusters of writers and examples of research that are used as references to support the description and commentary on a report. Often in journals, the use of particular writers as references is a better guide to the framework being adopted than the explicit statement made by the author. In many cases, more than one reference point is used by contributors to this book in order to highlight particular sets of issues.

Repertoires and dilemmas

The first reference point is that around the writers who have popularized discourse analysis in social psychology in Britain from the end of the 1980s (Potter and Wetherell, 1987; Billig *et al.*, 1988). Four of the chapters look to these writers. Moir (Chapter 2, this volume) takes up one of the issues explored in *Discourse and Social Psychology* (Potter and Wetherell, 1987), that of 'personality', and, in a careful analysis of the attempts at personality profiling used in psychological models of occupational career choice, shows how the talk both confirms *and* disconfirms just as strongly the idea that people in different career paths have certain personalities. Identifying what he calls 'linguistic repertoires', Moir uses Potter and Wetherell as one of his reference points to the power of conversational context on what people say about themselves from moment to moment. The lesson here is not only that the personality typing does not work, but that the phenomenon of personality itself is something which is a function of talk: it is as variable as talk. There is a short step from this point to the idea that questionnaire and interview responses are not tapping something outside language (or inside the head). As Moir points out: 'interview responses are therefore viewed as discursive practices and nothing more'.

Like Moir in his analysis of career interviews, Marshall and Raabe (Chapter 3, this volume) use the notion of interpretative repertoire, and look, as Potter and Wetherell (1987) do, to three crucial aspects of language. These aspects are that: (i) There is always a variation in the accounts that people give which is more important than the 'consistency' that psychologists usually fetishize; (ii) talk has a variety of functions other than that of simply transmitting information; and (iii) our talk and writing is constructed out of existing resources. These resources are the repertoires, repertoires we do not create anew when we speak, but which we have to borrow and refashion for our own purposes. A problem is that when we borrow a repertoire it always carries more with it than we (could) think. The second key issue that Potter and Wetherell home in on is attacked again by Marshall and Raabe, that of 'attitudes'. In their analysis of political talk, they show that the functions of the discourse are more important than underlying stable dispositions. As with the notion of 'personality', we are led to suspect that 'attitudes' are not fixed things inside the person but are a function of context and of repertoires.

Gill (Chapter 5, this volume) also locates her work with reference to the work on repertoires, but she augments this with a focus on the 'practical ideologies' that are called upon when people include or exclude others. The notion of 'practical ideology' is one that flows from the set of studies in the book *Ideological Dilemmas* (Billig *et al.*, 1988) where the 'ideological dilemmas' are those contrasting public and collective ideas that people negotiate when they weigh up, refer to and then discount alternative accounts. Thought itself, in this view, is 'dilemmatic', and Gill shows how the different accounts that radio disc jockeys give to justify the absence of women from radio are far from straightforward. As well as being another good example of how the traditional social psychological concept of 'attitude' will not work when we examine real talk, Gill's chapter shows how an attention to the multiple and contradictory reasons people give for their prejudice allows a better understanding of ideology than of simply delusion or fixed ideas.

Conversation and the making of sense

The second reference point would contest the notion of ideology as a set of fixed ideas, and would then go further than this to say that the 'repertoires' and 'dilemmas' that discourse analysis sometimes pretends to discover are themselves only creations of the analyst. Two of the chapters look to this reference point. Moir (Chapter 2, this volume) is cautious in his use of the notion of 'linguistic repertoire' because he also uses as his reference point writers in the sociological tradition of ethnomethodology (Garfinkel, 1967). Ethnomethodology is the study of the methodologies used by the 'folk' (hence 'ethno' — 'methodology') to make sense of the world, and for a researcher to pretend that they have 'discovered' the repertoires that govern what people say would be to do violence to what people actually say (and what they say they are saying). Moir wants to recover what sense his interviewees are making of the questions, rather than sum up what they are doing with a label he, the analyst, has imposed.

A sustained example of what is entailed by this approach is provided by Widdicombe (Chapter 6, this volume), who specifies two features of the analytic stance she adopts. While traditional sociological and social psychological accounts of subcultural identity claim to identify social forces or cognitive schemas which 'cause' people to develop particular identities, Widdicombe argues that identity is negotiated through talk. To capture some sense of the identity that a speaker or writer (or artist or sculptor or musician even, if we opened up our idea of what a text is) is constructing for themselves, it is necessary first to develop 'a sensitivity to the way language is used' and then to focus on the 'inferential and interactive aspects of talk'. The question she is asking as she picks through the interview transcripts are 'What problems are presupposed by the statements made here?' and 'What are the solutions that are being posed to those problems?'. While there is a reluctance to discover things (like repertoires and suchlike) in Widdicombe's work, the analysis is systematically organized around these questions. The rules of language use and meaning making are what are being elaborated here.

Structure and subject

A third reference point is that of 'post-structuralism' (Parker, 1989; Parker and Shotter, 1990). Here, the term 'discourse' is used instead of the term 'repertoire' (Parker, 1992). Post-structuralism is the term for an array of approaches which is suspicious both of claims to reveal a world outside language and of claims that we can experience any aspect of ourselves as outside language. Macnaghten (Chapter 4, this volume) uses the notion of ideological dilemmas and of argumentation with Billig *et al.* (1988) as his reference point, but he also wants to show that 'discourses' (a term he prefers to 'repertoires') imply social relationships. Reality, behaviour and subjectivity (our sense of ourselves) is always in a text. This is why post-structuralism provokes a deconstruction of the 'truths' we take as given, including the 'truths' about experience that are appealed to by religions or by humanism. Some writers using post-structuralism use the term 'postmodernism' to describe what they are doing – and this is the term currently favoured in the United States by social constructionists (e.g. Hare-Mustin and Maracek, 1988; Gergen, 1991). If this perspective is adopted, then any appeals to human nature, or other non-human nature must be rejected in favour of, as Macnaghten puts it: 'a research orientation based on a post-modernist commitment to *the socially constructed nature of reality*, or *the socially constructed reality of nature*'.

The term 'post-structuralism' still carries with it positivist echoes of its history in structuralism (an attempt to discover underlying universal structures to nature and culture), and Stenner (Chapter 7, this volume) therefore prefers to adopt an approach to the jealousy talk of his interviewees, which he calls a 'thematic decomposition'. His analysis of the narratives used by two people to construct themselves and their partner involves, as he says, 'a focus on the *storied* nature of jealousy' *and* (here is the post-structuralist reference point) a description of the 'subject positions' constructed in the talk for each person. When the post-structuralist twist to discourse analytic research is added, particularly in the use of Foucault's (1981) work, then we are able to look not only at how objects are constructed in discourse (objects such as 'personality', 'attitudes' and 'prejudices') but also at how subjects are constructed (how we experience ourselves when we speak, when we hear others speak about us, and how we still have to use that talk when we think without speech). Marks (Chapter 8, this volume) also uses post-structuralism as her reference point, and that, when combined with an attempt at radical action research, causes difficult practical moral/political dilemmas. We will return to this issue, but we want first to review moral/political advantages of adopting a discourse analytic approach.

MORAL/POLITICAL CONSEQUENCES OF DISCOURSE ANALYTIC RESEARCH

The 'turn to the text' has far-reaching implications for scientific, and especially social scientific, 'knowledge' (Gubrium and Silverman, 1989). There are three useful contributions that discourse analysis makes that we would like to draw attention to.

First, discourse analysis draws into psychology the work of Foucault (1972, 1980), and the way that foucauldian ideas have been used to provide a critical account of the function of the discipline of psychology itself. Rose (1985, 1990), for example, outlines how the definition and specification of the domain of 'individual psychology' arose within discourses of social regulation and classification emerging at the turn of the nineteenth century. This legacy can be seen in contemporary practices of developmental and educational psychology and personality theory. As Walkerdine (1988) points out, the effects of psychology's birth in the wake of Darwinian evolutionary theory, tied also to the modern programme of liberal reform, reverberate on theoretically in the celebration of rationality within models of development. They are also maintained by means of the normalizing practices (of health, law, welfare and education) which psychological knowledge informs. These accounts, following on from Henriques *et al.* (1984), have been used to problematize the effects of social scientific, and specifically psychological, practice by revealing it as participating within prevailing social norms and interests, historically and currently (Burman, 1991).

Second, drawing attention to the discursive structures of psychological accounts works to highlight the assumptions underlying them and challenges their facticity, that is, their status as truth. So, for example, Squire (1990) identifies three main discourses structuring psychological accounts: the detective narrative (driven by the need to find out and to solve problems); the autobiographical narrative (whose confessional and subjective qualities paradoxically work to reaffirm its objectivity and validity) and the science fiction narrative (which takes over at the fringes of psychological knowledge, engaging in 'speculative' and 'preliminary' investigations and foraying into new unknown territories). A consequence of this is that questions of theory and method become blurred (a familiar 'deconstructive' move), so that the critique applies to psychological tools as well as concepts. Potter and Wetherell (1987) correspondingly also couch their critique of psychological theory in methodological terms. They highlight how dominant psychological methods of, for example, rating scales that underlie attitude theory, fail to take account of the variability of human thought and action, and by doing so bolster a spurious model of thinking as uniform, rational, and classifiable into equal-interval categories. Hollway (1989) develops a version of this critique to import a psychoanalytic gender analysis, so that subjectivity and contradiction, long associated with the devalued and inferior thinking of women, come to be seen as not only inevitable features of, but also as vital for a more adequate understanding of, psychic life.

Third, the self-conscious attention to account and presentation, to context as well as content, gives rise to a focus on reflexivity. Reflexivity is seen as more than the condition of the psychological enterprise, of the reflective study of sentient beings. Reflexivity is also hailed as aiding accountability for discourse analytic readings by rendering interpretative resources and processes public and available for evaluation (Potter, 1988). Further, feminist uses of reflexivity have been concerned to draw attention to the participation of the researcher within research processes, and to the work of interpretation (Wilkinson, 1988). This is not simply to enrich the account, but to heighten questions of power relations in research. Focusing on meaning construction and the relationship between systems of meaning can facilitate an understanding of relationships between researcher and researched. This emphasis on the contradictions between discourses as well as their internal construction helps to theorize the functions they play within the social practices that give rise to them.

Marks (Chapter 8, this volume) highlights the way in which the contradictions between discourses are, in the research process, also contradictions between the researcher and those that psychologists normally call their 'subjects'. The focus in her chapter is on the power that operates in research, and the moral/political contradictions that beset someone trying to engage in 'action research'. Despite the concern with empowerment, and the giving of voice to the participants in the study, Marks shows, through a transcript of a meeting in which the analyses of an education case conference were 'fed back' to some of the original participants, that a foucauldian recasting of repertoires as 'discourses' cannot turn the study into one that is *necessarily* radical or progressive. What is disturbing about this account is that it is elaborating and reflecting on what is usually concealed in psychological research: what went on here is routine in traditional studies, but it patently is not enough simply to recognize the problem. This, perhaps, is an issue to do with the nature of discourse analytic research.

To summarize so far, an attention to discourse facilitates a historical account of psychological knowledge, mounts a critique of psychological practice by challenging its truth claims, and requires a transformation of our notions of what a good methodology should be like. This makes it possible to use the analytic framework to make interventions in the way psychology is constructed in culture. The current popularity of discourse analysis owes much to the ways its analytic tools can be used to inform political practice and struggles. So successful have these interventions been that discourse analysis is currently almost synonymous with 'critical' and in some cases 'feminist' research. Discourse analysis is used to comment on social processes which participate in the maintenance of structures of oppression. In psychology, for example, the approach has been used to analyse the workings of racist discourse (Potter and Wetherell, 1987; Wetherell and Potter, 1992) and to explore nuances and effects of such ideologically loaded and multiply determined terms as the 'community' (Potter and Collie, 1989).

A number of practical struggles can be informed by opening up the dilemmas wrought by the crossings and conflicts of discourses.

To take one example, the 'human rights' discourse of normalization in mental handicap recognizes gender-appropriate dress and behaviour as conferring full humanity in contemporary social life, but renders women vulnerable to abuse (Adcock and Newbigging, 1990). Another is how the discourse of 'protection' and 'innocence' in child abuse positions 'knowing' children as culpable (Kitzinger, 1988). Also, drawing attention to the teaching of children as occurring within specific discursive practices, such as game formats, that offer particular, gendered positions and that may be responsible for children's lack of progress (rather than some conceptual deficit), generates new strategies in education curriculum development and teaching practice (Walkerdine, 1988). As a final example, competing discourses of the child as 'having problems' rather than being 'the problem', call for contrasting outcomes which relate to decision-making processes in education case conferences (Marks, Chapter 8, this volume).

We list these examples to give a picture of how discourse anlaysis has been taken up in useful ways to inform political struggles. However, while there are historical connections between why and how discourse analysis has come to function as political critique (perhaps due to purposes and orientations of cultural analysts and importers of post-structuralist ideas), it is by no means clear that these political motivations guiding discourse analysis are necessary. Seidel (1986) and Barker (1981) highlight how the Right intervene in the field of discourse in a deliberate way, moving from biological theories of racial inferiority to discourses that appropriate the Left's celebration of cultural difference and pluralism, but add a new twist to treat difference as synonymous with inevitable conflict: conflict between cultural groups is then presented as resolvable only by compulsory repatriation. The fact that people of such different political standpoints can use discourse analysis could be seen either as an advantage or as a disadvantage. We look at some of the problems in Chapter 9 (this volume), but for the moment we want to draw attention to the need for a researcher to be clear *why* they are doing discourse analysis.

TENSIONS IN DISCOURSE ANALYTIC RESEARCH

If discourse analytic research is to be developed as an approach which *is* critical of psychology, and is not to be absorbed by the discipline as just yet one more 'method' in its armoury, we do need alternative spaces for theoretical debate and empirical work. Within the academic institutions, there are now many discourse groups, and their existence will be an important factor in the future shape of this area. All the contributors to this book have participated in the activities of the discourse analytic research group at the Manchester Metropolitan University, now the Discourse Unit – Centre for Qualitative and Theoretical Research on the Reproduction and Transformation of Language and Subjectivity.

We want to conclude this chapter by picking up points made by Figueroa and López (1991), in a review of a selection of recent discourse analytic research (including the chapters in this volume) in which they draw attention to tensions in contemporary discourse analysis. The tensions Figueroa and López identified were of four types. The first was a tension between the text and the context, in which there is the dilemma as to how far a researcher should go beyond the particular text they are analysing to arrive at an interpretation of what is happening. We need to know, for example, what the context is for the accounts that an interviewee is reported to have given, but when a researcher outlines this context, she is telling us more than the interviewee is saying in the transcript. How the text should be located by the researcher is a question that is addressed in different ways, and to varying degrees in the following chapters. The second tension is between discourse analysis which is effectively functioning as ideology-critique and traditional positivist methods masquerading as discourse analysis. Here the researcher may be wanting to use discourse analysis critically, in order to expose a particular set of statements as racist or sexist (as legitimating exploitation) and not succeeding. Alternatively, what looks like a critical discourse analysis may in fact be just an academic exercise with no progressive intention (or progressive effect). Deciding which is which is sometimes difficult for the reader (and slipping between one and the other may sometimes be a problem for the researcher).

The third tension is between the use of conceptions of power/knowledge and a range of other approaches which are simply descriptive. In some cases, the processes of power that are being referred to in the analysis may even be explicitly referring to foucauldian or feminist perspectives, while the actual 'analysis' does no more than redescribe what the interviewee (or other text) is saying. In some cases, the analysis may be a careful description and elaboration of implicit themes which need not necessarily be connected to an analysis of power and knowledge. The fourth and final tension is that between theoretically informed work (and here the frameworks may range from dilemmas in thinking and argumentation, to accounts of everyday reasoning, to post-structuralist theories of subject position) and research in which it appeared as if it were sufficient to let the data 'speak for itself'. The contributors to this book have discussed the theoretical frameworks they are using, but how far we connect our analysis to theory is a difficult question. In some cases we may want to simply offer the account to the reader, and it functions as an occasion to give others a voice. In some cases, it will be necessary to risk not being accessible in order to produce a deeper analysis which goes beneath what appears to be said.

There are no fixed answers to these tensions, these dilemmas in discourse analysis. They are there to be negotiated in the course of the research, and they are still there now for you to negotiate as you read them, as you turn to the text.

REFERENCES

Adcock, C. and Newbigging, K. (1990) 'Women in the shadows: women, feminism and clinical psychology', in E. Burman (ed.) *Feminists and Psychological Practice*, London: Sage.

Barker, M. (1981) *The New Racism*, London: Junction Books.

Billig, M., Condor, S., Edward, D., Gane, M., Middleton, D. and Radley, A. (1988) *Ideological Dilemmas: A Social Psychology of Everyday Thinking*, London: Sage.

Burman, E. (1991) 'Power, gender and developmental psychology', *Feminism & Psychology* 1 (1): 141–53.

Fairclough, N. (1989) *Language and Power*, London: Hutchinson.

Figueroa, H. and López, M. (1991) 'Commentary on discourse analysis workshop/conference', paper for Second Discourse Analysis Workshop/Conference, Manchester Polytechnic, July.

Foucault, M. (1972) *The Archeology of Knowledge*, London: Tavistock.

—— (1980) *Power/Knowledge: Selected Interviews and Other Writings 1972–1977*, Hassocks, Sussex: Harvester Press.

—— (1981) *The History of Sexuality*, vol. 1, Harmondsworth: Pelican.

Garfinkel, H. (1967) *Studies in Ethnomethodology*, New York: Prentice Hall.

Gauld, A.O. and Shotter, J. (1977) *Human Action and Its Psychological Investigation*, London: Routledge & Kegan Paul.

Gergen, K.J. (1991) *The Saturated Self: Dilemmas of Identity in Contemporary Life*, New York: Basic Books.

Gubrium, J. and Silverman, D. (eds) (1989) *The Politics of Field Research: Sociology Beyond the Enlightenment*, London: Sage.

Hare-Mustin, R. and Maracek, J. (1988) 'The meaning of difference: gender theory, postmodernism, psychology', *American Psychologist* 43 (6): 455–64.

Henriques, J., Hollway, W., Urwin, C., Venn, C. and Walkerdine, V. (1984) *Changing the Subject: Psychology, Social Regulation and Subjectivity*, London: Methuen.

Hodge, R. and Kress, G. (1988) *Social Semiotics*, Cambridge: Polity Press.

Hollway, W. (1989) *Subjectivity and Method in Psychology: Gender, Meaning and Science*, London: Sage.

Kitzinger, J. (1988) 'Defending innocence: ideologies of childhood', *Feminist Review* 28: 77–87.

Parker, I. (1989) *The Crisis in Modern Social Psychology, and How to End It*, London: Routledge.

—— (1992) *Discourse Dynamics: Critical Analysis for Social and Individual Psychology*, London: Routledge.

Parker, I. and Shotter, J. (eds) (1990) *Deconstructing Social Psychology*, London: Routledge.

Potter, J. (1988) 'What is reflexive about discourse analysis? The case of reading readings', in S. Woolgar (ed.) *Knowledge and Reflexivity: New Frontiers in the Sociology of Knowledge*, London: Sage.

Potter, J. and Collie, F. (1989) '"Community Care" as persuasive rhetoric: a study of discourse', *Disability, Handicap and Society* 4: 57–64.

Potter, J. and Wetherell, M. (1987) *Discourse and Social Psychology: Beyond Attitudes and Behaviour*, London: Sage.

Rose, N. (1985) *The Psychological Complex*, London: Routledge & Kegan Paul.

—— (1990) *Governing the Soul*, London: Routledge.

Seidel, G. (1986) '"Race", "culture" and "nation" in new right discourse', in R. Levitas (ed.) *The Ideology of the New Right*, Cambridge: Polity Press.

Squire, C. (1990) 'Crisis, what crisis? Discourses and narratives of "the social" in social psychology', in I. Parker and J. Shotter (eds) *Deconstructing Social Psychology*, London: Routledge.

Walkerdine, V. (1988) *The Mastery of Reason: Cognitive Development and the Production of Rationality*, London: Routledge.

Wetherell, M. and Potter, J. (1992) *Mapping the Language of Racism: Discourse and the Legitimation of Exploitation*, Hassocks, Sussex: Harvester/Wheatsheaf.

Wilkinson, S. (1988) 'The role of reflexivity in feminist psychology', *Women's Studies International Forum*, 11 (5): 493–502.

Part I

The textual construction of psychology

Chapter 2

Occupational career choice: accounts and contradictions

James Moir

This chapter looks at the application of discourse analysis to the study of occupational-choice accounts. The utility of this approach will be demonstrated through an examination of vocational under-graduates' responses on being interviewed about their course and related occupational choices. The analysis of these responses is located within an attempt to provide an empirically demonstrable critique of traditional psychological approaches to the study of occupational choice. These traditional approaches have sought to use respondents' answers as a means of revealing underlying psychological structures or processes which govern occupational choice. Discourse analysis does not attempt to reveal psychological universals but rather is concerned with the social context in which responses are generated and, in the case of interviews, the interactive functions they may serve (Potter and Wetherell, 1987).

There have been two main psychological approaches to the study of occupational choice. The 'personality-matching' approach has primarily relied upon psychometric testing in order to predict occupational choice on the basis of personality assessments. Foremost amongst those taking this approach has been Holland (1959, 1985) who has formulated a personality typology based on preferences for particular kinds of work. Six types are specified in terms of work-related interests and aversions. Realistic types are said to prefer working with objects and machines and do not like educational or therapeutic activities. Investigative types value systematic study, usually of a scientific nature, and do not like working on repetitive tasks or in situations where they must deal with others. Artistic types are said to value activities which are creative, and to have an aversion for systematic or fixed kinds of work. Social types prefer to work with people and do not like tasks involving machines or tools. Enterprising types like to work in situations where they can persuade or manipulate others and do not like investigative activities. And finally, conventional types are said to prefer working with records or data and to have an aversion for free, unsystematic activities. 'Personality patterns' represent particular combinations of the six basic personality types and are expressed in terms of a two- or three-type code. A person is said to be consistent if the elements of his or her subtype share common characteristics, and inconsistent if they are conflicting. 'Subtypes' represent the personality patterns that are prevalent in particular occupations.

The second main approach is the 'developmental' approach which has primarily used interview responses to identify stages in the maturation of vocational thinking. Accordingly, occupational choice is viewed as a process which takes place over several years, the underlying theme of which is the maturation of our capacity for 'realistic' (i.e. rational) occupational decision-making. In the first comprehensive theory of this kind (Ginzberg et al., 1951) three stages were specified: (i) the fantasy stage (from approximately 6 to 11 years of age) during which children express their occupational preferences in terms of those occupations which seem glamorous or adventuresome; (ii) the tentative stage (from approximately 11 to 17 years of age) during which there is a growing awareness of both internal (e.g. interests and abilities) and external (e.g. employment opportunities) factors that will affect the outcome; and (iii) the realistic stage (17 years of age and over) during which stock is taken of past decisions and particular occupational fields are investigated leading to a commitment to aim for a specific kind of job.

Another important researcher in this area (Super, 1957) has also formulated developmental stages which emphasize the development of an individual's work-related self-concept across the life span. One of his main contribution has been the identification of 'developmental tasks' related to vocational development and his notion of an individual's 'vocational maturity' (i.e. the rate and progress made towards 'realistic' occupational decision-making).

Now that we have some purchase on the traditional psychological approaches, in the next section we will turn to looking at the alternative discourse-analytic perspective to the studying of occupational-choice accounts.

INVESTIGATING OCCUPATIONAL-CHOICE DISCOURSE

If the interactive nature of interview dialogue becomes the focus of study, then one must give up attempts to view responses as indicative of certain types of 'occupational personality' or as revealing a respondent's stage of 'vocational maturity'. Instead, the central question becomes: How do respondents attempt to produce coherent and credible accounts of their occupational choices? In order to accomplish this analytic task we must look at the kind of accounting practices used to justify occupational choices. In other words, we must look at what Potter and Wetherell (1987) refer to as the 'linguistic repertoires' which respondents draw upon. In this context these repertoires can be thought of as the broad kinds of account that respondents draw upon when talking about their course and related occupational choices.

It is important to note here that responses are not viewed as revealing respondents' 'real' reasons for choosing particular occupations. As Garfinkel (1967) argues, we account for our decisions in a retrospective manner. As such, decision-making may have little to do with electing a course of action on the basis of available information but rather may be the product of our ability to define the basis for decisions once made. This type of accounting can therefore be viewed as justifying a course of action and involves 'assigning outcomes their legitimate history' (Garfinkel, 1967: 114). Interview responses are therefore viewed in terms of discursive practices.

The extent to which certain types of accounts are regarded as credible will depend upon the way in which respondents interpret the interviewer's questions and also the way in which the interviewer receives their responses. The ways in which respondents attempt to understand what the interviewer is 'looking for' can be approached from a conversation analytic viewpoint. From this perspective the interview can be thought of as a series of question-and-answer sequences (cf. Sacks, 1972). These exchanges are usually under the control of the interviewer who can use respondents' answers to generate further questions. Respondents must therefore attempt to gauge the direction and import of questions in the course of hearing them and be responsive to the interviewer's line of questioning.

An analysis of question-and-answer sequences in interviews allows the researcher to see the way in which the language game is played back and forth until a point is reached where the interviewer regards a particular question topic as having been answered satisfactorily. This can be achieved by noting when new question topics are initiated. In other words, it is possible to look at the success or failure of particular linguistic repertoires by examining the extent to which the interviewer pursues a respondent's initial answer to a question topic and the extent to which the interview runs 'smoothly'.

The analysis of interview transcripts in this chapter was based on a study involving forty vocational students from two degree courses at Dundee Institute of Technology: mechanical engineering and nursing undergraduates. These groups were selected because: (i) their course choice represents a choice of a specific occupational domain; and (ii) conventionally, they are thought of as attracting very different individuals, thereby allowing for the contrast of different linguistic resources with regard to 'personality-expressive' discourse.

The interviews were conducted using an interview schedule and were tape-recorded. The transcription of this material stresses readability and does not feature, for example, intonation or pause lengths. Such a detailed level of transcription was not necessary given that the analytic focus was directed at the content of the linguistic repertoires drawn upon by respondents. The transcripts are coded, for example: 1NRS3 represents year 1, nursing, respondent number 3; and 5ME9 represents year 5, mechanical engineering, respondent number 9. Where the tape recording could not be heard clearly this is shown in the transcript as (inaud.).

'Personality-expressive' accounts

Looking for personality types

According to the 'Occupations Finder' in Holland (1985), mechanical engineering comes under the category of 'realistic' occupations. It is therefore said to attract people who primarily perceive themselves as having practical abilities and a preference for working with objects and machines rather than people. Realistic types are also said to be materialistic, valuing money, power and status. The particular sub-type for this occupation is specified as 'realistic, investigative, enterprising'. The investigative element being of secondary importance is associated with a preference for intellectual work and an interest in science. The enterprising element is what Holland refers to as the tertiary element of this particular personality profile, and is associated with a preference for work where leadership or an ability to influence others is required, as in managerial or sales positions.

General nursing comes under the category of 'social' occupations. It is therefore said to attract people who primarily perceive themselves as having interpersonal skills and an aversion for systematic, ordered work involving objects or machines. The particular subtype for the occupation of general nurse is specified as 'social, investigative, artistic'. 'Investigative' is the secondary element of this subtype, implying the preferences mentioned above whilst the artistic element refers to a preference for unstructured creative activities and an aversion for systematic work (as is found in 'conventional' occupations, e.g. a clerk).

The following extracts show typical responses which appear to accord with Holland's typology for these occupations.

5ME9 (male, 23)

Int: Why did you want to enter the field of mechanical engineering?

Resp: Well, it just started off from being an interest when I was young, making models from *Meccano* kits and mechanical subjects at school, I quite enjoyed them. I enjoyed the physics, maths side of it. I wasn't certain I wanted to do mechanical; there's civil, electrical and chemical. I just had a look around and decided to come to the mechanical course.

1NRS7 (female, 17)

Int: Why do you want to go into the field of nursing?

Resp: I think it will be a well worth job, I'll get a lot of job satisfaction from it and every day is going to be different, it's not going to be boring. And getting to know more people and helping them, feeling that you're doing something at the end of the day, it's not just wasted really.

The mechanical engineering respondent (5ME9) traces his choice back to an interest in construction kits and 'mechanical subjects at school'. This appears to indicate a preference for 'realistic' activities. He then goes on to mention that he enjoyed physics and maths, that is, 'investigative' subjects. This response therefore appears to reveal the first two elements of the mechanical engineer subtype. In contrast the nursing respondent (1NRS7) expresses a preference for working with people and helping them, and for variety of work. This response appears to correspond to the 'social' and 'artistic' elements of the nurse subtype.

Conversational complexities: disappearing types

Although it was possible to select responses which seemed to offer support for Holland's personality types for these occupations, it became evident that this could only be achieved by ignoring the complex conversational context of such responses. When this was examined, mismatches between responses and the typology were revealed and categorization often became problematic. Indeed it can be said that the 'types' tended to disappear into the discursive fabric weaved by researcher and respondent.

As the following respondent's answers show, variability of response can undermine attempts to apply Holland's apparently straightforward categorizations.

5ME10 (male, 25)

(1)

Int: Why did you want to enter the field of mechanical engineering?

Resp: Well it's a subject, engineering as a whole is a subject that I've been interested in since a child, building things, seeing how things work, taking things apart. And also there's the influence of my parents, my father's an architect and also my grandfather's an engineer, so there's a sort of family thing. So no matter how much you try to get away from it you are influenced by what your parents do. But generally from an early age I was interested in machines and it stemmed from there.

(2)

Int: How did you arrive at your particular decision to aim for this occupation?

Resp: Em, well funnily enough I did a year of architecture before starting here. I was always interested in building something, design, that sort of area, construction. So I tried architecture and discovered that midway through that year I wasn't interested in it. So I completed the year and came here.

In extract (1) the respondent links an interest in practical activities he engaged in as a child ('building things' and 'taking things apart') with an interest in machines. This appears to be a straightforward instance of a 'realistic' personality type. However, in extract (2) the same interest is associated with design and his earlier choice of architecture. 'Building things' and 'construction' are now associated with an interest in buildings. Yet Holland classifies architecture under 'artistic' occupations, a type which is unrelated to engineering! Had a brief structured interview or questionnaire been used to explore respondents' views of their occupational choices this 'qualification' might not have emerged. However, the conversational nature of the interview reveals a complex account of occupational choice which is not easily reduced to Holland's discrete categories.

'Personality traits' and membership categories

I have pointed out that some responses on the face of it appear to offer a degree of support for Holland's view that personality directs occupational choice. The mechanical engineering and nursing respondents did after all refer to very different kinds of reasons for their choices. Mechanical engineering students tended to mention a preference for working with machines and an interest in maths and physics at school as the basis for their choice, whereas the nursing students tended to mention a preference for working with people and helping them. It could therefore be argued that underlying personality traits are revealed by these very different kinds of account. However, an alternative perspective emerges when we consider the production of these accounts as fulfilling an interactive function.

One way of investigating connections between occupations and personality traits is to consider these as the articulation of our conventional knowledge of membership categories (Sacks, 1972, 1974). It must be stressed that these categories, although stocks of conventional knowledge, are nevertheless linguistic devices used in the accomplishment of meaning-making and deployed by speakers for specific purposes (i.e. linguistic repertoires). So why do respondents draw upon these standard membership categorizations when talking about their choice of occupation rather than a specialized knowledge? An answer to this question can be found by looking at differences in the sequences of talk between those who use these kind of responses early on in the interview and those who do not. Consider the following pair of extracts.

5ME9 (male, 23)

Int: Why did you want to enter the field of mechanical engineering?

Resp: Well, it just started off from being an interest when I was young making models from *Meccano* kits and mechanical subjects at school, I quite enjoyed them, I enjoyed the physics, maths side of it. I wasn't certain I wanted to do mechanical engineering, there's civil, electrical and chemical. I just had a look around and decided to come to the mechanical course (inaud: several secs).

Int: Do you think there are any particular qualities required to be a mechanical engineer?

1NRS7 (female, 17)

Int: Why do you want to go into the field of nursing?

Resp: I think it will be a well worth job, I'd get a lot of job satisfaction from it, and every day is going to be different, it's not going to be boring. And getting to know more people and helping them, feeling that you're doing something at the end of the day, it's not just wasted really.

Int: What drew you to nursing? You could speak to people in other jobs, why nursing?

Resp: Because you're helping them, they're not able to do something themselves so then you've — without being there they would have a harder time even though maybe they're not ill, just to speak to you and understand how they feel or if they are ill to get them through that stage.

Int: Did you consider any other careers?

These extracts are examples of the 'standard membership category repertoire' for choosing these occupations. Respondent 5ME9 mentions the 'realistic' and 'investigative' elements of the mechanical engineer subtype: an interest in construction kits and mechanical subjects at school, and an interest in science. Note how once this response is given, the interviewer begins a new question topic. Two question-and-answer turns are required to establish the 'social' and 'artistic' characteristics of respondent 1NRS7. Her first answer stresses the importance she attaches to working with people, and for variety of work. The interviewer asks her to be more specific and she obliges by elaborating about helping people. The interviewer moves on to another question topic after this response, thereby indicating that it is satisfactory.

These short conversational exchanges can be contrasted with the protracted question-and-answer sequences of the following extracts which draw upon the 'family influence repertoire' of accounting for occupational choice.

5ME2 (male, 21)

Int: Why did you want to enter the field of mechnical engineering?

Resp: Well, my brothers all did engineering so I was kind of led onto that when I left school and I had been brought up to go along (inaud.). I'd always been interested in engineering, cars and motorbikes and stuff like that so it was just there wasn't any other option and I just went straight into it. I wasn't really thinking career-wise what particular area I wanted to go into, it was more or less it was engineering or nothing else.

Int: When you say there was nothing else, why did that arise then? Did they talk to you, or did you feel this was the right area for you?

Resp: Well, it was the right area for me anyway and I'd thought of other careers, you know you go through the range of them and engineering seemed to be the only reasonable one because I took to it quite naturally, with machinery and stuff like that, so I thought I'd may as well just continue in that line rather than tackling something else and finding that I wasn't cut out for it.

Int: Did your brothers tell you what it was about?

Resp: Well I had a fair idea. I realize now that I was a wee bit limited in my knowledge of what it covered, the whole range of subjects it covered, you know, thermodynamics and that sort of stuff. And most of the subjects aren't that interesting, there's only a few specialist subjects that I find interesting. But if I had done something different, say civil or electrical or something like that, I knew that I wouldn't be as happy as I am just now because I don't find electrical that interesting and difficult to undertstand; similar with civil. So if I had to choose now I would have still made the same choice.

Int: What is it that draws you to mechanical as opposed to electrical or civil?

Resp: Well when I was younger my brothers always had some kind of machinery. There was motorbikes and cars and engines and stuff like that which I took to quite readily. Very little electrical work came into it or structural work and I'd always felt it easier on the mathematical side of the subjects in school, the physical sciences rather than the other subjects, you know, literature or things like that.

Int: When you say working with machines, motorbikes and cars, is that mechanics then?

1NRS8 (female, 19)

Int: Why do you want to enter the field of nursing?

Resp: 'Cause I've always had an interest in it from when I was young (inaud.). My mum had been a nurse and I have lots of relatives who are nurses and they all sort of, not influenced, but I was always interested in what they had to say about their work. And I just like being with people but I didn't want to be stuck in an office and didn't want to be stuck in a shop or anything 'cause I've worked in a shop and I know what it's like, it's alright doing it part-time but it's not for me to be able to enjoy it. And, I just wanted to a be a nurse 'cause I like people, that's the main reason.

Int: You say there's people in your family who are nurses. Did they influence you, did they talk to you?

Resp: When they'd come home they'd talk about their work and things like that, that's more or less it and that's it I said I was going to be a nurse and no arguing about it. I think mum was a bit surprised 'cause I'd never said anything when I was younger, that I wanted to be a nurse 'cause usually you say you want to be something when you grow up and it changes every week but with me it's that I've always wanted to be a nurse and I think she was surprised that I was going through with it.

Int: When you say you've always wanted to be a nurse what is it then that has attracted you to this area? You say you like working with people but I could give you many jobs where you would be working with people, why specifically nursing?

Resp: It's more personal with the person being a nurse, it's not sort of working on a shop counter and saying 'that's £50 please!' That person means nothing to you. And I know you're not meant to get personally involved with your patients but you still have an interest in them whereas other jobs (inaud.) to me, maybe you are, maybe other people think different but to me you're really interested in the person.

Int: But I could give you a job where you're interested in people, let's say a school teacher or lecturer. Now there you have an interest in your pupils or students, you're talking to people, you're helping them learn. I'm interested in why you want to do nursing, I mean you've mentioned your relatives and it would seem to me that they held sway with you, a great influence on you.

Resp: Well, teaching for a start wouldn't be for me because I couldn't stand up and tell them (inaud.), it's not for me.

Em, I've thought about all them things but I've always sort
of swayed towards nursing.

Int: What other careers did you think about?

Respondent 5ME2 begins by talking about the influence of his
brothers who had taken up engineering before him. Respondent
1NRS8 points out that her mother as well as her other relatives
are involved in nursing. In both interviews the interviewer pursues
the extent to which the respondents were influenced in their choices.
In both cases the respondents detect the import of this questioning
and respond by referring to their long-standing interest in their
intended occupations. In answering this question, respondent 5ME2
claims that he had 'thought of other careers' thus contradicting what
he had said in his initial response that 'there wasn't any other option
. . . it was more or less engineering or nothing else'. Thus, external
influences on his choice are played down and he now appears to
have made a considered decision. He is then able to refer to his
interest in machines as the deciding factor in his choice. At this stage
respondent 1NRS8 still refers to her family members who would
'talk about their work' but is careful to point out that it was she
who decided upon nursing ('I said I was going to be a nurse and
no arguing about it' . . . 'I've always wanted to be a nurse').

Despite these responses which refer to the independent nature of
the respondents' choices, they are pursued further about the nature of
their decisions. After being asked about the information he received
from his brothers, respondent 5ME2 is asked about the specific branch
of engineering he chose to enter. It is at this point that he draws
upon the 'standard membership category repertoire'. Thus, he again
refers to his experience of working with machines but also adds that
he was interested in physics and maths at school. In the interview
with respondent 1NRS8 the interviewer challenges her to be more
specific about her choice of nursing by providing other examples
of occupations that involve working closely with people. However,
unlike the engineering respondent she does not refer to any interests
or preferences 'characteristic' of nurses but answers the question in
a direct manner by providing a reason why she is unsuitable for
teaching. She then reiterates her long-standing interest in nursing.
In both cases the interviewer gives up the line of questioning and
moves on to another topic.

From this analysis we can see that the justification of occupational
choice in terms of a 'standard membership category repertoire' is

more readily accepted by the interviewer than a 'family influence repertoire'. Furthermore, an account which although referring to the independence of the decision made is nevertheless still probed further to elicit the basis of the choice, that is, the 'personality' of the individual. Respondents who therefore 'collude' with the interviewer and refer to characteristics they possess conventionally associated with their chosen occupation establish their suitability for such work, whereas respondents who refer to the influence of others in their choice, what has been called the 'family influence repertoire', leave this to be established. It is therefore no wonder that the majority of respondents justify their occupational choices using the 'standard membership category repertoire'; conversationally, it is much easier and leads to a 'smooth' interview.

Looking at 'developmental' discourse in dialogue

The maintenance of 'realistic' accounts

Respondents were often asked 'follow-up' questions, particularly on the basis of their responses to the opening question. This in effect set respondents the task of attempting to maintain their choices as 'realistic' across succeeding question-and-answer turns. Thus, choice realism can be viewed as a construction which emerges and is maintained through the question-and-answer sequences of the interview. This can be illustrated through the analysis of the following extract involving a mechanical engineering student.

1ME6 (male, 17)

Int: Why do you want to enter the field of mechanical engineering?

Resp: Because I think it strongly relates to the subject I'm best at, physics. I've always enjoyed this kind of work, maybe not exactly the same thing, but working on cars, motorbikes and things. It's a slightly higher that's all.

Int: When you say you enjoy working with cars and motorbikes is this a hobby?

Resp: Yeah, more of a hobby.

Int: And what sort of things do you do then?

Resp: Eh, just (inaud.) some cars and things, just basically help my dad service the car.

Int: Yeah, but I could say then that is surely being more of a mechanic than a mechanical engineer.

Resp: I realize that but I'm maybe slightly more intelligent, more able to become a mechanical engineer as opposed to a time-served mechanic.

Int: Do you see any difference between what a mechanic does (*Resp:* Oh yeah) and a mechanical engineer? What is the main difference then?

Resp: Well a mechanic is more using his hands to repair whereas a mechanical engineer might possibly design as opposed to repair.

Int: Is this an area you're interested in, design?

Resp: Yes, that's what I put on my application form. I hope to go into design at the end of the five years, if I get five years.

Int: You say you're interested in physics, why then not take up a career involving physics?

Resp: I'm not that deeply into the subject, I always like to broaden my horizons, not get narrow-minded into physics. I did consider doing physics certainly, but I feel this is the better subject to do.

In his answer to the opening question Respondent 1ME6 refers to his ability in physics which he points out is related to mechanical engineering In the remainder of his answer he links mechanical engineering with 'working on cars and motorbikes and things' although he claims the former is at 'at a slightly higher level'. His claim to have 'always enjoyed this kind of work' would appear to perform a similar function to that mentioned in the previous section, namely to demonstrate through a long-standing interest, his vocational commitment and suitability for the job. Indeed, the nature of this interest is checked upon by the interviewer's next two questions and the respondent's answers would appear to confirm the impression of his choice as arising out of his mechanical interests.

However, the interviewer subsequently throws a metaphorical spanner in the works by challenging the respondent to distinguish the sort of work he has mentioned and that of being a mechanical engineer. The respondent then justifies his mechanical engineering choice by claiming that he is 'maybe slightly more intelligent' than what is required for a 'time-served mechanic' training. The interviewer's next question shows that he regards the respondent's answer as either incomplete or vague since he rephrases the challenge, this time as a direct question requiring the respondent to distinguish between the two. At this point the respondent differentiates the two occupations in terms of 'repair and design'. The interviewer then picks up on the respondent's reference to design work and the respondent substantiates his interest in this aspect of engineering by mentioning he had put down an interest in this kind of work on his application form. The next question shifts the conversation back to the respondent's declared interest in physics and challenges him to provide a rationale for choosing mechanical engineering over a career more directly concerned with physics. The respondent now plays down his interest in this discipline by claiming that he is not 'that deeply into the subject' and that he does not want to be 'narrow-minded'.

By unravelling the nature of the dialogue between interviewer and respondent we can see how the appearance of 'realistic-stage' discourse has been sustained. This involved a number of qualifications and variations in the description of his choice, but over a sequence of turns different responses achieve a coherent overall impression of rational decision making.

'Fantasy stage' responses as functional

Although all of the interviews were dominated by 'realistic-stage' responses there were cases where respondents also talked in a manner that could be categorized as revealing 'fantasy-stage' thinking. From a developmental perspective this causes something of a problem as it undermines the hypothesis of normative age-graded vocational thinking and of distinct developmental stages. However, an examination of the conversational context in which these responses were given again provides an alternative explanation.

An example of this can be seen in the answers given by several of the nursing respondents who claimed that they had 'always' wanted to be a nurse or had done so from an early age.

1NRS8 (female, 19)
Resp: . . . usually you say you want to be something when you grow up and it changes every week but with me it's that I've always wanted to be a nurse . . . .
Int: What other careers did you think about?
Resp: Em, other jobs in hospitals.
Int: Such as?
Resp: Radiography, then I thought I don't have physics so I put that out of it. And then there's occupational therapy and

physiotherapy and I thought no, I want more personal contact with the patient rather than in and out really.

4NRS3 (female, 21)

Int: When you say you always wanted to do that, was there any particular reason for that? Was there anyone in your family . . .

Resp: No, em well I've got a couple of cousins and things that are nurses but not really very many. But I think when you say you're always wanting to be an air hostess, and a teacher, and a nurse, and I just never got away from that . . . .

The claim 'I've always wanted to be a nurse' can be thought of as a useful way of establishing a respondent's vocational commitment in an occupation that is commonly associated with dedication and the ideal of service. However, when faced with a question which appears to demand a 'realistic-stage' answer, respondent 1NRS8 obliges by referring to occupations she claims to have considered along with her reasons for rejecting them in favour of nursing. There is no conversational contradiction here. The respondent successfully communicates commitment and rationality.

Responses like those above make it difficult to assume that an underlying mental capacity (i.e. 'realistic' thinking) is responsible for occupational choice. Rather, it is the ability to meet the demands of the interviewer's questions and present one's choice in a credible manner that is being displayed.

CONCLUSIONS

It was noted that a fundamental assumption underlying the psychological approaches is that respondents' answers, whether in the form of psychometric test responses (the mainstay of the personality-matching approach) or interview responses (the mainstay of the developmental approach) can be used as the basis for respectively categorizing personality types and levels of vocational maturity. I have argued that 'personality-expressive' and 'realistic' accounts are a product of accounting for occupational choice, that is, they are discursive practices. I have also argued that some linguistic repertoires (e.g. the 'standard membership category repertoire') are more successful than others (e.g. the 'family influence repertoire') in terms of their persuasiveness in establishing a respondent's suitability for a particular occupation. The linguistic repertoires which interviewees draw upon are therefore a key consideration in the production of a convincing account. This point will be developed later with respect to careers guidance.

An alternative approach to the study of occupational choice accounts has therefore been demonstrated; one which examines the influence of the interactive context on the way respondents construct their answers. This perspective enables an examination of the functions respondents' answers serve and allows the researcher to study the whole conversational pattern of the interview transcript and not just those parts which can be extracted and categorized according to a particular theoretical framework. Thus, we have seen how some responses simply do not fit with Holland's personality typology and how respondents can also draw upon 'fantasy' as well as 'realistic-stage' responses. In effect, these difficulties to cope adequately with the conversational context in which responses are generated calls into question the psychological reality which these theories purport to describe. They may be based on results which are artifactual due to the decontextualized manner in which they are analysed.

It is important to note that the kinds of response that have been looked at in this chapter were not produced as a result of attempts to elicit them through prior theorizing before students were interviewed. The questions asked of students were drawn from the researcher's own unexplicated common-sense notions about what should be asked in exploring course and related occupational choices. It was only as a result of analysing the question-and-answer sequences in the transcripts that these notions were exposed and called into question. These notions are of course reflected and formalized in the two main psychological perspectives on occupational choice.

It is also important to note that no claim is being made that the analyses that have been offered are the only interpretations that are possible. Potter and Wetherell (1987) point out that a major advantage of discourse analysis is that the presentation of transcripts along with the analytic claims affords the reader the opportunity to evaluate those claims. Whether or not one agrees with these claims, the focus remains on discursive functions and the common-sense assumptions which underpin the dialogue.

The personality-matching and developmental approaches to occupational choice have had an important influence on careers guidance. Guidance based on the 'appropriate-personality' view attempts to match individual attributes to what are regarded as appropriate occupations. This type of guidance usually operates with clients who are faced with imminent career decisions. The techniques used can vary but there is generally a reliance upon psychometric measurements. The developmental approach to guidance is more long term and is aimed at facilitating 'vocational maturity'. Much emphasis is placed upon the notion of careers education and counselling clients through interviews in order to help clients attain 'realistic-stage' decision making.

However, if we are concerned with the interactive nature of interview dialogue, then it can be argued that a central concern of those involved in careers guidance should be equipping clients with the conversational skills required for employment interviews. A conversational-skills approach to career preparation, focusing upon the practice of those linguistic repertoires found to be successful in interviews, would also have the advantage of recognizing the agency (rather than the 'personality' or 'maturational' limitations) of candidates. Responses could be practised in a role-play situation and audio and video feedback techniques could be used to confront clients with their shortcomings.

Some advice for interviewees on bringing off successful occupational-choice accounts can be given based on the analysis of the transcript extracts of this chapter. In general, interviewees should establish early on their suitability for their chosen occupation using the 'standard membership category repertoire'. It is also important that interviewees 'collude' with the interviewer so as to produce a 'realistic' decision-making account. It is not possible to plan the deployment of these repertoires in interviews in any detailed way since they must be drawn upon to meet the demands of particular questions (cf. Suchman, 1987). However, it might be possible to provide interviewees with some practice in adapting these broad kinds of account.

By this point the reader may be asking, will not this emphasis on learning to say the 'right thing' undermine the use of interviews as a means of selection? There is plenty of evidence pointing out the weaknesses of selecting personnel through interviewing (see, for example, Herriot, 1987). Despite this, interviews continue to be one of the main techniques of personnel selection. Perhaps this is because interviewers draw upon common-sense notions that interviewees' answers reveal something of their personality characteristics and motivations for applying for a particular post (or vocational course in the case of course-selection interviews). If one abandons this assumption and instead views selection interviews in terms of discursive practices, then there can be no doubt that the adoption of such a perspective will lead, not only to a questioning of the use of selection interviews, but also of our faith in the 'reality' that there are 'personality types' which are best suited to particular occupations.

REFERENCES

Garfinkel, H. (1967) *Studies in Ethnomethodology*, Englewood Cliffs, NJ: Prentice Hall.

Ginzberg, E., Ginsburg, S.W., Axelrad, S. and Herma, J.L. (1951) *Occupational Choice: An Approach to A General Theory*, New York: Columbia University Press.

Herriot, P. (1987) 'The selection interview', in P. Warr (ed.) *Psychology at Work*, Harmondsworth: Penguin.

Holland, J.L. (1959) 'A theory of vocational choice', *Journal of Counseling Psychology* 6: 35–45.

—— (1985) *Making Vocational Choices: A Theory of Vocational Personality and Work Environments*, 2nd edn, Englewood Cliffs, NJ: Prentice Hall.

Potter, J. and Wetherell, M. (1987) *Discourse and Social Psychology: Beyond Attitudes and Behaviour*, London: Sage.

Sacks, H. (1972) 'An initial investigation of the usability of conversational data for doing sociology', in D. Sudnow (ed.) *Studies in Social Interaction*, New York: Free Press.

—— (1974) 'On the analysability of stories by children', in R. Turner (ed.) *Ethnomethodology*, Harmondsworth: Penguin.

Suchman, L. (1987) *Plans and Situated Actions: The Problem of Human Machine Communication*, Cambridge: Cambridge University Press.

Super, D.E. (1957) *The Psychology of Careers*, New York: Harper & Row.

Chapter 3

Political discourse: talking about nationalization and privatization

Harriette Marshall and Bianca Raabe

Traditionally, psychology's concern with political issues has taken a narrow focus defining 'political' mainly in terms of party politics and assuming that individuals hold consistent political viewpoints which can be measured using attitude scales. These make way for the categorization of participants into political 'types'. Many of these psychological scales and surveys rely on detailed statements expressing an opinion to which respondents register their level of agreement or disagreement (see for a recent example, Jowell *et al.*, 1990). The statements only provide opinions towards certain topics, in some cases as set within a specific context (for example, 'If people worked hard at their jobs, they would reap the full benefits of our society' (Christie *et al.*, 1968)). However, the use of propositional statements has been criticized as being inadequate on the basis that the initial emotional response of the subject would be tempered by consideration of the qualifications and justification posed in the statement (Wilson and Patterson, 1968). It has been suggested that this form of statement hinders the respondent because they feel committed to providing a rational and considered judgement.

The question of context is the key focus here. The perspective taken by traditional approaches to measuring political attitudes was that respondents would be unable to express an opinion on an issue unless provided with a specific context. Wilson and Patterson (1968) clearly saw this as a limitation and proposed that if attitudes were to help with the prediction of behaviour, it was necessary to measure the affective (emotional) stage and not the cognitions (as the traditional approach has done). As a result they abandoned propositions replacing them with a list of brief labels representing familiar and controversial issues, for example, patriotism, apartheid and socialism, upon which they assumed people hold clear-cut views.

Consequently, their scale is drawn up of fifty words with no context provided. The researchers considered that participants' responses to these words allowed for individuals to be measured and categorized in terms of their 'conservatism' or 'liberalism'.

The assumption that these attitudinal studies share is that there is some enduring entity within individuals that can be measured. Potter and Wetherell (1987) reject this assumption and argue that when people fill in an attitude scale, their responses should not be thought of as indicating a pathway to some internal attitude, but instead thought of as specific linguistic formulations which are dependent on specific contexts. Further, while attitudinal research concentrates on consistency, seeing it as indicative of descriptive validity, a discourse analytic approach examines regularities in the linguistic resources used by participants. Consistency at the level of discourse is then viewed as a product of the function to which the discourse is put.

There is a further way in which discourse analysis studies differ from traditional attitudinal studies. Rather than attempting to restrict participants' responses, in terms of allowing only one response to a number of statements or items, it is seen as important that participants should discuss in full their ideas and understandings of the issues of concern. If this is allowed, then variation will emerge both due to the complexity of the issues explored and due to the functions of the discourse. This is the perspective that we will take in this study in working with in-depth interviews and allowing participants to discuss the issues of concern as fully as they wish.

Finally, this discourse analytic study differs from traditional studies in its perspective on language. While attitudinal research sees language as an essentially colourless, transparent medium, unproblematically describing some underlying 'real' entity, discourse analysis takes language as actively constructing versions of the social world. Given that there are a number of ways in which any issue or event can be described, and that participants select linguistic resources out of a pre-existing pool, discourse analysis examines the linguistic resources made use of by participants. The important point here is that some ways of describing, making sense of, certain issues are so familiar, so 'obvious' that they appear to be 'common sense'. The fact that they are a construction, one particular version, is obscured.

In this chapter we will examine the ways in which participants discuss privatization and nationalization, traditionally associated with the 'right and left' political viewpoints (Dunleavy, 1979). We will

later consider the possible political consequences of the constructions used. What we are concerned with here, in this preliminary
study, is how discourse of events and beliefs is manufactured (see
also Hollway, 1989; Marshall, 1991; Potter and Reicher, 1987). The
intention is to demonstrate how the meaning and use of political
concepts vary according to context and as related to purpose. A main
aim is to reconsider the attitudinal research by allowing participants
to explore various considerations of privatization and nationalization which, we argue, problematizes the assumption that individuals
can be placed exclusively into one political category in the way that
attitudinal researchers, including Wilson and Patterson, would
suggest.

BACKGROUND TO THE STUDY

Participants

Sixteen people known to one of us, took part in the first part of
this study. Participants came from a range of occupational backgrounds including graphic designer, psychiatric nurse, factory shift
manager, pensioner, teacher, student and business consultant. Their
ages ranged from 28 to 65 years. Participants were living in three
areas of England: London, Norwich and Birmingham. They were
first asked to complete Wilson and Patterson's 'New measure of conservatism' (1968). The two items of concern in the second part of
the study – those of nationalization and privatization – were added
to this scale. Using Wilson and Patterson's criteria the five highest
scorers were categorized as 'conservatives' and the five lowest scorers
as 'liberals'. These ten participants then took part in the second part
of the study and were individually interviewed.

Interviews

Interviews comprised eighteen questions concerning various aspects
of privatization and nationalization. The questions were broadly structured into four sections: section A, general questions about privatization; section B, general questions about nationalization; section C,
questions concerning specific contexts and industries in relation to
privatization and nationalization; and section D, general questions
about the handling and future of privatization and nationalization.

The interviews were carried out in informal settings, mostly in the homes of the participants. Two were carried out in an interview room in a psychology department of a London polytechnic. Each interview lasted between 30 and 45 minutes and was tape-recorded and transcribed.

The analytic process followed was basically that set out by Potter and Wetherell (1987). The identification of recurrent patterns in the linguistic constructions, referred to here as repertoires, was tackled by reading and rereading the transcripts and taking out instances where there appeared to be terms, phrases or metaphors linked to the concepts of privatization or nationalization either in terms of (i) similarity in structure or content; or (ii) differences or variability in what was being said. Extracts were initially taken out if they seemed even loosely associated with each concept. This process was repeated a number of times, first, placing extracts under broad headings such as support for privatization, support for nationalization, rejection of privatization or rejection of nationalization. Second, attention was given to how the selected constructions were being used and whether they seemed to serve the same function. Finally, for the purpose of this study, consideration was given to the relationship of repertoires to the 'liberal' and 'conservative' categorizations of participants according to Wilson' and Patterson's (1968) categories.

Each extract is preceded by 'C' or 'L' indicating categorization of participant as 'conservative' or 'liberal' respectively, followed by participant number. Instances where an ellipsis (. . .) is present in the extract indicates the material does not follow on directly. Interviewer's questions are prefixed with 'Int' to separate them clearly from participants' responses.

ANALYSIS

In the analysis which follows, two main repertoires are outlined – 'efficiency' and 'social justice', with attention given to how participants categorized as 'liberal' and 'conservative' using Wilson and Patterson's scale, make use of these repertoires. It will be demonstrated that the repertoires are not exclusive to any particular political viewpoint and that they function to allow participants to rationalize or disclaim privatization or nationalization, depending upon the context.

Efficiency

The repertoire that dominated 'conservative' participants' discourse about privatization was that of 'efficiency'. This was used by four out of the five 'conservative' participants throughout their interviews. The extracts below provide some examples to outline this repertoire.

'Conservative' participants' use of 'efficiency'

Int: What do you think are the important arguments when discussing privatization?

C5: Getting industries to run efficiently, getting rid of bureaucracy which doesn't really operate industry to the benefit of the population. The best way to get the industry working for the population is to get it working for profit.

C4: You see if you provide better competition, it's bound to improve the price which you are going to pay for products. Also of major importance is efficiency. The trouble with nationalized industry is that it's totally inefficient and ineffective.

C2: There are certain sections like, a good example would be council refuse. I think that's a good thing to be privatized and I think it has been, in a lot of councils and they've found that not only is it sort of cheaper, but it's more efficient and I think there are certain things like schools where there are certain sections that could be privatized which are not.

Int: Are there any other arguments concerning privatization even if you don't necessarily subscribe to them?

C5: Well some people say that it's wrong to privatize things that belong to the people but I think that's completely misplaced really because, okay, the government owns resources but by transferring them to the private sector then we can get them actually running more efficiently.

In all these extracts 'efficiency' is characterized as being a good thing and it is discussed as though it is taken for granted that it is equated with privatization. In the second extract a clear link is constructed between inefficiency and nationalization. What is meant by efficiency is not made explicit in that no participant attempts to define what this term means, and therefore it could refer to increased profits for industry, or improved service or production as a result of restructuring, again either for the service providers or the consumers. The function of the 'efficiency' repertoire in these extracts is quite clear: it serves as a justification for the support of privatization.

Variability in 'conservative' participants' use of the 'efficiency' repertoire

A given participant will often use the 'efficiency' repertoire in different ways, this is illustrated in this section using extracts from one account (C2). Over a range of questions 'efficiency' is first brought up to support privatization, then to negate it, and finally to support nationalization.

Int: What do you think are the effects of privatization?

C2:   Well what are there, efficiency covers a real wide scope doesn't it in respect of the efficient running so you get a better service for whatever industry or thing it is and a lower cost.

Int: Other effects?

C2:   Oh yes, it's very impersonal, whereas you get state industries, old Fred's been a doorman of a certain hospital, or a porter and regardless of what he's done over the years he's always been there because that's his job and nobody would ever give him the sack. Whereas in private industry the efficiency and the very thought that if he were surplus to requirements he'd have been sacked years ago. . . . We now have in Birmingham not just the West Midland Transport that used to be Birmingham corporation, we now have private coach firms which run along the same routes as the West Midlands go and, once again now I think that where they belong to West Midland travel, before they were probably more efficient.

Int: Are there any other arguments you can think of when discussing nationalization?

C2:   Privatization of the right type of industry or service can be beneficial, it has some good points. A good example of what a state–owned industry should be is the rail service. I think that should remain as a nationally owned one, because if it can't run efficiently and make a profit that's just too bad. What is the main thing is that it provides a service for the public.

Clearly when the 'conservatives' discuss privatization, the first thing that springs to mind is efficiency. However, as noted earlier, efficiency is not clearly defined, but nevertheless used as if it is the telling argument. As the participant continues to discuss privatization disquiet emerges, as to whether the main concern should be efficiency, or whether there are other things to consider such as lack of social concern, 'impersonality', as discussed with respect to 'poor old Fred the doorman'. Furthermore, it becomes very diffcult to determine what efficiency means when as illustrated in the above extract, a service is characterized as being unable to run efficiently, and cannot make a profit yet is apparently identified as being more desirably nationalized: at this point the 'efficiency' repertoire is no longer useful and is abandoned.

The 'efficiency' repertoire as used by 'liberal' participants

The 'efficiency' repertoire was also used by three out of five participants in the 'liberal' group when they discussed nationalization. However, the use of the term 'efficiency' is somewhat different from that of the 'conservatives', as these extracts demonstrate:

Int: What do you think are the important arguments involved in the issue of nationalization?

L2: Obviously the other side of privatization, how best to, if something is a nationalized industry then how best to, how most appropriately, how most efficiently that's the word I'm looking for, for the sake of the industry and for the sake of those working in the industry, how to manage it . . . . If you are making sure that water for people's drink is clean, then that would take priority, but the people working within the industry, yes, how to serve the public how to look after the people that are working within the industry and how to run it efficiently and not waste public money.

L1: In some instances, of course, price is neither here nor there. Certain provisions need to be made such as the National Health Service. I think if it was run properly on a nationalized basis then, you could have equal efficiency and innovation.

The 'efficiency' repertoire is used in these extracts in association with a number of different social concerns, in terms of doing the best for the industry, for those who receive the product or service and for those working within the industry. Although 'efficiency' is considered to be an important criterion in the running of industry, no presumption is made that privatization equals efficiency and nationalization equals inefficiency. It would appear that the objective here is to break the link betweeen privatization and efficiency.

This is clearly demonstrated by the following extract which seems to drive a wedge between the association of privatization and efficiency.

Int: Are there any other arguments you can think of concerning privatization?

L2:   I hear arguments about when people are pro privatization about efficiency, avoiding waste as public service industries seem to be very good at wasting time, man power, resources or at least accused of those things. When I hear those arguments about needing competition to increase efficiency there's something in me which wants to say well, yeah, that may be true but there has to be ways of increasing efficiency without moving the power behind the control of those industries into privatization, into private hands.

In this extract as in the 'conservative' participants' use of this repertoire, 'efficiency' is identified as a good thing. But while 'efficiency' is used as a criterion to assess the running of industries, it is not assumed to be linked to privatization. Thus 'efficiency' is proposed but with the suggestion that this could be in association with nationalized industries.

The 'social justice' repertoire

A second repertoire, while not as evident as that of 'efficiency' was drawn on in a number of the interviews. The 'social justice' repertoire refers to the needs of the people, and discusses the importance of ensuring a good service, in the form of 'protection', good working conditions for those in the industry and a fair deal for those receiving the service or the goods.

The 'liberal' participants' use of the 'social justice' repertoire

The majority of 'liberal' participants made continued reference to certain services being best left in the public sector, because of social concerns, over and above 'efficiency' as the extracts below demonstrate. This repertoire was used repeatedly by 'liberal' participants to argue in support of nationalization and against privatization as the following extracts demonstrate:

Int: What do you think are the effects of nationalization — beneficial or otherwise?

L2:   What are the benefits of nationalization? Well hopefully if the government is doing its job, control of that service, providing a good service, providing protection for the, good circumstances, situation for the people working within the service, putting money gained, resources gained back into the service, that sort of thing.

L1:   I think it can achieve a balance in where the money goes, whether things are cost-effective, whether certain things are not cost-effective but necessary, so it provides a better service for the people receiving it and the people who are working within it.

The above extracts illustrate how the repertoire of 'efficiency' is overruled by that of 'social justice' when discussing certain industries or services. Here some services are characterized as being 'essential' or as providing 'basic necessities' which are said to be better nationalized.

Int: What arguments do you think are important in the issue of nationalization?

L1:   How best the state can provide essential services to the public at the best possible price. In some instances, of course, price is neither here nor there. Certain provisions need to be made such as the NHS. I think if it was run properly on a nationalized basis then, you could have equal efficiency and innovation.

Int: Are there any state-owned services which you think ought not to be privatized?

L5:   Well you know water is one of the basic necessities of life and it just seems awful to me that water can be privatized. Again the same sort of argument as far as I'm concerned as before, that water has already been paid for by the tax payer, and now we're being asked to buy shares .... I mean in the Midlands there were sort of funds raised years ago apparently, to pay for the water to be brought into this part of the country from Wales and I just don't like the whole sort of feel of that. And as I say for such a basic thing that we all need to survive.

L3:   I think in an ideal world I don't think health, education, funerals, anything that everybody in life needs, which is silly because everyone needs heat as well.

Int: Are there arguments for nationalization?

L3:   Yes again it's back to providing of services as cheaply as possible equal services. Providing services where they are needed to people who actually need them regardless of their ability to pay.

In the above extracts the participants use a moral language suggesting that 'the people' should have 'equal rights' to certain essential requirements, necessary to their survival, although as seen in extract three above there is ambiguity in the definition of what services are 'needed'. The distinction between 'necessary services' and others is used to argue in favour of nationalization. This argument is used not only by 'liberal' participants but also by 'conservatives' to justify support for nationalization.

'Conservative' participants' use of the 'social justice' repertoire

The following extracts show how the 'conservative' participants abandon privatization in favour of nationalization using the 'social justice' repertoire as justification. In a similar way to that demonstrated in the 'liberal' participants' accounts, the 'conservatives' make repeated reference to the need to provide essential services being better served by nationalization. There is clearly a shift to an alternative 'moral' argument which concerns itself with public welfare. Participants indicate that there is a moral obligation for the state to provide certain requirements because it serves the nation.

Int: What do you think are the important arguments in the issue of nationalization now and for the future?

C1:   I think if nationalization, going back to the railways, I think they should keep it and they should invest more money in it because it's such a public service, rather like the French have done.

Int: Are there any state-owned services which you think ought not to be privatized?

C2:   There aren't so many these days are there? I feel all the services should remain nationalized, gas, water, electricity, railways. Anything which serves the nation, provides a service.

Int: What issues do you think are important when discussing nationalization?

C3:   Those things that are giving a service, which ... that isn't going to be profitable and never will be, that gonna need investment from the people rather than giving people the option of whether to invest you need to make compulsory investments like through national insurance. So things like the medical service where there's loads of it that just won't be profitable and never could be, but you need that service because it's going to affect people who wouldn't be able to afford it themselves therefore you need to insist that people pay and that everybody should pay, but that's the only real thing . . . . Basically all those services that are, it comes back down to what I class as essential. It's all the non-profitable services that society expects like health, someone to keep an eye on the law, someone to sort of, community services like that, mainly that sort of thing, that's the best description of nationalized services.

As demonstrated earlier the 'conservatives' use 'efficiency' to justify their preference for privatization. However, they will abandon the use of this repertoire taking up the provision of 'essential services' and public 'need' to justify support for nationalization. The third extract in particular points to an idea posed on many occasions that government provision is needed because the industry would not be profitable on its own. However, while the 'conservatives' use the 'efficiency' repertoire, to argue that privatization results in efficiency, inconsistency in the argument emerges as the 'social justice' repertoire is used to argue that certain services, although inefficient are better served by nationalization. What is evident is that there is *not* unconditional support on the part of 'conservatives' for the privatization of all industries and services.

The following extract shows how variability occurs within one participant's account about nationalization and privatization, resulting in inconsistencies within an argument.

Int: Why are you against privatization of British Rail and water?
C1: Well, because they ought to be a public service and I'm not sure industries like that, that everybody relies on the way we do on the national health service should be privatized. Because you are going to get a big divergence maybe of interest, and also the cost going up as in water, our water is disgusting anyway. It's going to cost a lot to put that right, that's one particular thing I feel strongly about. The railways are the other. We ought to be like France where they've got a fantastic railway system. But the government injects a lot

of money into it. But as for other things like the hospitals I think they do need some sort of privatization.

In this extract the participant questions whether the National Health Service should be privatized because it is a public service and one which everybody 'relies on'. To justify supporting national control of the railways, reference is made to France, which is seen to provide a good nationalized service. This is explained as being due to government providing the funds. At the end of the extract a contradiction occurs: the recommendation is made for some form of privatization of hospitals, there is clear variability here.

It should be noted that although there is support for nationalization, certain parameters are set as to how far nationalization should go. The function of efficiency, as used by the conservatives, is to support privatization. However, in certain contexts this is then dismissed as not important.

The justification of privatization by 'liberal' participants

Finally, it can be shown that in the 'liberal' participants' discourse there are means by which they support the idea of privatization. In the following extracts the circumstances under which privatization is considered to be acceptable are discussed:

Int: How about food production and car production? How far would you go with state control?

L2:   Production of goods like cars, right, production of material goods. I might at this stage leave that in the hands of private enterprise I think. The control of basic services I'd leave in the hands of the government.

Int: Are there any goods or services which you think it is appropriate for the state to provide?

L1:   Health, water, the fundamentals of life. To give everybody an equal opportunity, yes I think the state should provide anything like that. I like the idea of the state being in control of everything which is national, of things which are a factor in every person's everyday life. I can come to terms with things which are or don't concern everybody being in private hands, so people can have a choice as to whether to use those facilities or not.

In the previous two extracts, privatization is justified by drawing on the notion that some goods are not essential nor part of

everybody's lives and therefore can be handled best by the private
sector. Again, the emphasis for nationalization is on the provision
of essentials or the 'fundamentals of life'. In the first extract a clear
distinction is drawn between material goods as appropriate for the
private sector, and basic services better left in the hands of the
nationalized sector. In the second extract the suggestion is that those
areas that don't concern everyone can be left to the individual to
choose whether they want them or not. The shifts between
nationalization and privatization can be seen in the following extracts.

Int: How about food production?
L5: Well I would prefer it not to be really. It's so sort of widespread
and diverse isn't it that I feel it's probably beter handled by
individuals. That's not to say that in some cases to encourage
farmers along the lines of growing crops that are necessary
and not so profitable that they shouldn't have subsidies and
everything. No I can't see the gain in having food and farming
nationalized.

This extract raises the question about whether food production is
not 'necessary', 'essential to survival' as used by this same participant
to argue for nationalization earlier in the same interview. The definition produced earlier that industries which produce 'essential goods'
which are used by everybody, are better nationalized, is not
sustained here. Other 'liberals' can be seen to draw on arguments
against nationalization, discussing the disadvantages of the loss of
individual enterprise and reliance on the system as justifications.

Int: How far would you go with nationalization?
L4: There's a drawback with nationalization inherent in socialism
where everybody starts to rely on state infrastructure . . . the
system to supply all their wants and needs and the kind of
initiative starts to drop out of the window so you get very
little change. You have to leave enough latitude for individual
activity even in areas as apparently boring as food supply or
water supply. You have to leave certain latitude for initiative.
Without it there's no improvement in the services you're
supplying.
Int: Initiative in what sense?
L4: You'd have to go into particular examples I suppose . . . bread
production. I mean if the government specifically dictated that
a specific governmental loaf was to be produced, there would

> be a huge vested interest in maintaining the governmental loaf and no-one would have invented granary bread or croissant. That applies right across the board even with water supply, you can't have Perrier water.

In the above extracts, nationalization is rejected for various reasons. First, on the basis that some areas are too diverse and therefore best dealt with by individuals, thus implying privatization is appropriate here. The second extract points to what are considered to be problems of nationalization, making people too dependent upon the state and removing initiative. The suggestion is that nationalization leads to stagnation and loss of individual creativity. It must be noted, however, that while nationalization is not totally rejected it is characterized as not appropriate in all cases.

In considering the above extracts it can be seen that participants do not hold consistently onto their notions of privatization and nationalization at all costs. Participants from both groups accept or reject both notions, depending upon the context in which they are placed. They dip in and out of the available discourses in order to make sense of the issues at hand. It seems that there are two 'moral' arguments at work here. The morality of privatization, which involves 'efficiency', is its most important characteristic for the conservatives. 'Efficiency' is also considered important for the liberals but is not necessarily constructed as being equated with privatization. The alternative 'moral' approach concerns the provision of basic needs and services needed by the public as voiced in the 'social justice' repertoire which, while not as prevalent as the 'efficiency' repertoire is made use of not only by 'liberals' but also by 'conservatives'.

DISCUSSION

Discussions of privatization and nationalization in these interviews were examined in relation to the pre-categorization of participants as 'liberals' or 'conservatives' using Wilson and Patterson's scale. Having outlined the 'efficiency' and 'social justice' repertoires we have analysed the ways in which each repertoire is used. 'Efficiency' is used to set up an association with privatization and as such functions as justification for privatization, but then 'liberal' participants, also drawing on the importance of 'efficiency', break the link between privatization and 'efficiency'. Instead a notion of 'social justice' is drawn on to argue for nationalization with both 'liberal' and 'conservative' participants constructing a distinction between 'essential services' and material goods. What is clear is that neither 'conservatives' nor 'liberals' give unconditional support for either privatization or nationalization, respectively and inconsistencies can be seen clearly in all the accounts. As different aspects of privatization and nationalization are explored, the criteria used to discuss the conceptualizations shift. In order to make sense of, or justify the seeming contradictions, participants dip in and out of available discourses. What is quite clear is that asking an individual to respond to single words or even statements with agreement or disagreement is inadequate.

In this study, one main aim was to question psychologists' reliance on notions of consistent attitudes in researching political issues. In several cases we have pointed to the way a particular participant makes use of repertoires. It could seem as though we are seeking to link individual participants with particular repertoires, which is not our intent. Rather, we see it as important to make clear that the focus of discourse analytic research is on regularities in the construction and function of linguistic resources and a move *away* from the individual as the unit of analysis. Our analytic attention to the *variety* of discourses used by each participant is important at the level of theory as well as of method.

There are a number of problems and limitations that have become clear in using discourse analysis, some of which arise with any research, and some specific to this study. In general terms, the idea of 'letting discourses emerge' and not imposing a structure on the analysis is problematic. Many attempts to follow through what appeared to be patterns in the constructions and functions, proved fruitless. Further, only two repertoires are outlined here. There were other repertoires we have touched on but not analysed in detail, for example, concerning 'individual choice' and 'individual enterprise'.

Further, for the most part our concern with the consequences of the discourse has been examining justifications, disclaimers and the construction of certain distinctions in definitions. We have given little consideration to large-scale political consequences. We would see it as important and emphasize the need to engage in the debate around these same issues in a macro-context, at the societal and political level.

The recurring use of two repertoires, in particular the 'efficiency' repertoire which was drawn on repeatedly by the majority of participants, points to the limited linguistic resources drawn on by participants. Relatively narrow parameters are set as to how to make sense of these complex issues. This raises the question as to what conceptualizations are currently missing from the debate. It is at this point that consideration of the need for the articulation of new discourses becomes relevant. Deconstructing existing conceptualizations makes way for a reworking and construction of new discourses as a means towards political change.

It has been argued elsewhere that through the 1980s British society and values have shifted to the right (Gray, 1990). Further though, and related to this study, political language has changed so that a core set of ideas emanating from the new right are used to justify the changing social and economic policies (Hall and Jacques, 1989). These 'core beliefs' include the desirability of individual enterprise, and the importance of reducing dependency on the state (Hamnett et al., 1989). We would argue that the repertoire of 'efficiency' as linked with privatization is part of this construction.

Related to this point, it should be noted that we have carried out an analysis which is concerned with everyday understandings. However, we have not tackled the question of where these understandings come from. What is also important is to examine the discourses around the same issues in the public domain, for example, at the level of policy and governmental debate. It is at this point that the question of power becomes of immediate concern, where the focus turns to examining agencies who hold the power to decide the terms within which such issues are to be discussed, and the means to circulate and perpetuate particular discourses. This relates closely to debates concerning 'political' bias in the media. We would argue that as well as considering whether certain political parties are allowed greater access to media coverage, that it is crucial to examine the parameters set by the media in the discussions of political issues, including nationalization and privatization. In these ways discourse analysis draws attention to the constructive effects of language use and can thus take the form, not only of political commentary but also of intervention.

REFERENCES

Christie, R., Friedman, L. and Ross, A. (1969) 'New left scale', in J.P. Robinson and P.R. Shaver (eds) *Measures of Social Psychological Attitudes*, Michigan: Institute for Social Research, University of Michigan.

Dunleavy, P. (1979) 'The urban basis of political argument: social class, domestic property ownership, and state intervention in consumption processes', *British Journal of Political Sciences* 9: 409–45.

Gray, J. (1990) 'Conservatism, individualism and the political thought of the new right', in J.C.D. Clark (ed.) *Ideas and Politics in Modern Britain*, London: Macmillan.

Hall, S. and Jacques, M. (eds) (1989) *The Politics of Thatcherism*, London: Lawrence & Wishart.

Hamnett, C., McDowell, L. and Sarre, P. (eds) (1989) *The Changing Social Structure*, London: Sage.

Hollway, W. (1989) *Subjectivity and Method in Psychology: Gender, Meaning and Science*, London: Sage.

Jowell, R., Witherspoon, S. and Brook, L. (eds) (1990) *British Social Attitudes, the 7th Report*, Northants: Gower.

Marshall, H. (1991) 'The social construction of motherhood, a discourse analysis of childcare and parenting manuals', in A. Phoenix, A. Woollett and E. Lloyd (eds) *Motherhood: Meanings, Practices and Ideologies*, London: Sage.

Potter, J. and Reicher, S. (1987) 'Discourse of community and conflict: the organisation of social categories in accounts of a "Riot"', *British Journal of Social Psychology* 26 (1). 24–39.

Potter, J. and Wetherell, M. (1987) *Discourse and Social Psychology: Beyond Attitudes and Behaviour*, London: Sage.

Wilson, G.D. and Patterson, J.R. (1968) 'A new measure of conservatism', *British Journal of Social and Clinical Psychology* 7: 264–9.

Chapter 4

Discourses of nature: argumentation and power

Philip Macnaghten

This chapter will give an account of a discourse study looking at how the category of 'nature' was constructed in a public inquiry. It will attempt to reveal four different constructions of nature: the process in which they were strategically used as arguments; and the relationship between argumentative strategies and existing sources of power. This analysis is theoretically novel in that the analytic unit used was not a 'repertoire', defined in terms of grammatical construction but a 'discourse', defined in terms of implied social relationships.

Although nature has long concerned people, there can be little dispute that the concept of nature recently has been gaining significance. Indeed, in a world threatened by atmospheric warming, acid rain, deforestation and global pollution, it is increasingly difficult to escape arguments which concern nature and our relationship to it. Not surprising then, that psychologists are beginning to wake up to the importance of this construct as it relates to human behaviour.

TRADITIONAL PSYCHOLOGICAL RESEARCH ON NATURE

I will begin by briefly describing existing research by psychologists on nature. This research will not be looked at in terms of content but in terms of its assumption that nature exists as a given entity, a priori defined as wilderness.

Often when we think about nature, we think conceptually about a world which is disappearing, about places in danger of being lost, about places that used to exist everywhere but which rarely do now. And it is this concept which is taken as given in much contemporary psychological work on nature.

Specifically, nature is assumed to be a *given, singular entity*, and to exist only in areas which have been *untouched by humanity*; places defined as undisturbed virgin areas or wilderness. The extract below is a typical example of a piece of research which implicitly makes this assumption through the synonymous use of the term 'nature' with 'wilderness': 'Both wilderness users and non-users have been found to share perceptions that experiences in natural environments can be highly satisfying and can offer valuable psychological benefits not found elsewhere' (Talbot and Kaplan, 1986: 177).

The assumption that nature can be a priori defined as wilderness has led psychologists to equate psychological research on nature with research which focuses on the psychological importance of wilderness's to human behaviour and functioning. To date, this research now includes: how natural environments are specified (Wohlwill, 1983); the factors which predict preferences of natural environments (Kaplan *et al.*, 1972; Herzog, 1987; Ullrich, 1983); developmental studies on nature (Ullrich and Ullrich, 1976; Wohlwill, 1983); and the psychological benefits of nature (R. Kaplan, 1977, 1984, 1985; Talbot and Kaplan, 1986).

This assumption depends on the acceptance of the *ontological* premise of realism – the premise that there exists a world separate from human experience. This premise is taken on board through the assumption that a natural environment exists whether we exist or not, and through the definition of nature as wilderness. However, the above research on nature not only proposes that natural environments exist by virtue of their untouched status, but also that we gain knowledge of them *vis-à-vis* this status. As such, the research presumes *epistemological* as well as ontological realism.

A DISCOURSE STANCE

While it is difficult to summarize exactly what is the discourse stance, one aspect shared by a variety of discourse approaches is the assertion that all forms of social reality have a peculiarly human and socially constructed nature. Put in philosophical terms, while discourse theorists may be ambivalent to the virtues of realism in ontological forms (i.e. the possiblity of a reality which exists separate from human activity and experience), they share a rejection of realism in epistemological terms. In other words, they share an assumption that 'knowledge of' can never be knowledge of an *extra*-human dimension (e.g. a world of science, objective fact, etc.), as all knowledge is irretrievably connected to a reality – produced, bounded and sustained by human meanings and constructions. Ibañez (1991) describes how this 'postmodernity' promotes an essentially *human* quality in experience:

> Post-modernity asserts that everything that is produced by human beings is irremediably and unavoidably just *simply human* that is, contingent, variable, relative to historically-changing human practices and ways of life. That means that we can find nowhere outside our own productions to check their value, for the standards used to check them stem themselves from our own productions. . . . These criteria are nothing other than *human products* and, *as such*, they are tied to human contingent decisions as well as being historically bounded.
>
> (Ibañez, 1991: 8, original emphasis)

This postmodernist's *constructivist* and *historical* commitment (i.e. the assertion that all accessible reality is both humanly constructed and historically bounded) leads to a heightened emphasis on the means through which human meanings and experience are manufactured –i.e. that of discourse. Here, a post-structuralist use of the term 'discourse' is deployed in which it refers not only to observable linguistic activities, but also to the world of human signs, symbols, activities, texts, etc. which together comprise a particular world view. As such, discourse analysts (or at least those who employ a postmodernist epistemology) tend to assume that our experience of reality is constituted in and through discourse, and that the aim of analysis is to unravel the processes through which discourse is constructed, and the consequences of these constructions.

INTRODUCING THE DISCOURSE ANALYSIS

The discourse analysis to be described in this chapter will use a research orientation based on a postmodernist commitment to *the socially constructive nature of reality, or the socially constructed reality of nature.*

While the theoretical aims of the analysis were broadly in sympathy with the theory on discourse analysis as set out by Potter and Wetherell (1987, 1988), Potter *et al.* (1990), Wetherell (1986) and with the approach to rhetoric and argumentation as set out by Billig (1987, 1990), the theoretical orientation did differ from that of the aforementioned authors in relation to analytic unit. Specifically, the disagreement relates to the proposal held by the aforementioned

theorists that discourse is constructed by our selective use of 'repertoires'. The disagreement lies not in the assertion that there exist
analytic units of discourse which we use to manufacture text, nor
in the assertion that different repertoires engender different outlooks,
but in the assumption that a repertoire can be *primarily* located in
grammar.

For the aforenamed authors, a repertoire is identified by
grammatical constructions: by way of particular narrative forms,
metaphors, tropes and common places which occur stereotypically
when we discuss certain topics:

> Any particular repertoire is constituted out of a restricted range
> of terms used in a specific stylistic and grammatical fashion. Com-
> monly these terms are derived from one or more key metaphors
> and the presence of a metaphor will often be signalled by certain
> tropes or figures of speech.
>
> (Wetherell and Potter, 1989: 172)

This approach is criticized in its primary emphasis on grammar. An
alternative analytic unit, named a 'discourse', will be used, which
becomes identified in terms of the *social relationships* it implies and
the *human uses* it legitimates. This alternative is argued to be more
appropriate to the process of conducting a discourse analysis since
it identifies the analytical unit at the level of social function as
opposed to the level of individual grammar. Discursive constructions obviously use grammar but what lies central to each construction is not the use of the same grammatical terms but the social relationship encapsulated by these terms, the outlook they engender,
and the activities they legitimate (whether these will be achieved
or not depending, however, on the process of argumentation).

The research objectives are set out as follows. The first aim was
to analyse the text in terms of the *variety* of different constructions
of nature used. The concept that different constructions exist and
are used in discourse is in direct contradiction to the assumption
in existing psychological research that nature exists as a given
entity, a priori defined as wilderness.

The second aim was to identify how these constructions of nature
were used as *argumentative strategies*. For example, some of the
arguments were contesting 'what nature was', while other arguments
related to whether a particular case was a legitimate or illegitimate
example of nature. In other words, the former arguments related
to contesting the essence of a construction of nature, while the

latter arguments related to whether the particular case in dispute could legitimately be categorized in terms of a particular construction of nature.

The third aim was to link the different constructions of nature to the different realities legitimated. The idea that language is *productive* is also in contradiction to a realist epistemology which assumes that language is separate from the human-independent world it addresses. A discourse epistemology alternatively assumes that language can *actively produce* a social reality as well as describe it. In this analysis, the use of different constructions of nature will be related to what they legitimated in terms of human relationships and uses.

And the final aim of the analysis was to look at the relationship between the argumentative strategies in terms of the constructions of nature used, and the material outcome of the discourse. This was achieved by first, linking the different argumentative strategies to existing structures of power, and second, by showing how the material outcome was based both on arguments which were bounded by these structures, and also by arguments which contested these structures.

INTRODUCING THE PUBLIC INQUIRY

The discourse analysis is related to a public inquiry concerning a planning application for a landfill site (or tip) to be sited on the outskirts of a city. The application had been turned down initially by the county council on landscape grounds. The public inquiry was attended by council officials and communuity groups on one side; by the developers on the other and presided over by a government-appointed inspector.

This particular inquiry was chosen as the basis for a discourse analysis first, because it involved arguments contesting the category of nature, and second, because it was a good example of how this struggle of words would have very real material consequences. Indeed, to the developers there was at stake a business valued in millions, while for the local authorities and local communities there was at risk all the potential nuisances that would result from land-filling activities as well as the changes that would occur to the physical shape of the environment.

The main body of text used for the discourse analysis was based on the spoken and written text given in the inquiry. This text included the written evidence of the main participants, the subsequent cross–examination by the opposing party and the inspector, and the final report written by the inspector comprising his findings. This was also supplemented by interviews with the main participants.

The transcripts were based on the written evidence, all the spoken text from the seven interviews and chunks of text selected from the tape-recordings of the public inquiry. The decision to select extracts from the total recordings of the inquiry was made since much of the inquiry related to technical details which bore little or no relevance to the category of nature. However, at this early stage of the analysis, every piece of text which could have been inter-preted in some way as relating to the topic of nature was included in the transcripts. From the twenty-six original tapes, six tapes of selected data resulted.

Before attempting analysis, a process of coding began. The coding was simply an attempt to distinguish the bodies of text which surrounded the topic of nature from those which didn't.

It has to be acknowledged that some examples of the topic were more implicit than others. For example, many arguments used a particular construction of nature without making the term 'nature' explicit. The identification of the implicit as well as the explicit usages of constructions of nature was perhaps the most difficult part of the discourse analysis. The process of determining a coding system which allowed for this possibility lay first, in locating where the term 'nature' was used explicitly, and second, in identifying the *social relationships* implied along with the grammatical constructions which encapsulated these relationships. And when the constructions had been located via explicit usages of the category, coding procedures then also included those constructions where the same implied relationships were used but where the actual term 'nature' was not. Having highlighted all the examples where constructions of nature were used, the procedure of coding moved into the process of analysis.

DISCOURSE ANALYSIS: THE RHETORIC OF NATURE

The main findings of the discourse analysis will now be discussed in three parts which broadly relate to the four objectives as set out. The first will locate the four different constructions of nature used (objective 1) in the inquiry and the argumentative strategies used within these constructions (objective 2). The second part will look at the argumentative strategies which made use of differing

discursive constructions (objective 2) and the third part will look
at the relationship between the argumentative strategies used in the
inquiry, the external constraints to the discourse and how these were
related to the final outcome (objectives 3 and 4).

In this chapter there will be a number of extracts taken from the
transcripts. To save repetition, abbreviations will be used. 'D' will
stand for the developers, 'C' will stand for the council officials and
'I' will stand for the inspector. To refer to the source of the extracts
the abbreviations 'W' will refer to written evidences given at the
public inquiry, 'S' will refer to spoken cross-examination and 'V'
will refer to the interviews. The extracts will be numbered in
numerical order.

Discourses of nature and how they were argued over

In terms of argumentative strategies over nature, the broad options
open to both the developers and council officials were interpreted
as follows. To the developers, there are two main strategies available:
either they could argue that the existing site was already *separate from
nature* and that their proposals would either restore the naturalness
of the site or have no *real* effect, or they could argue that the site
was a bona fide part of nature that would be unchanged by their
proposals.

For the council officials, the options are limited to one clear
strategy: that the existing site is a good and legitimate *part of
nature*, and that the impact of the appeal proposals would change
the categorical status of the area from the natural to the unnatural.

Nature as wilderness

The first discourse located in the text was named 'nature as
wilderness'. It was located via a variety of grammatical constructions including the labels: virgin, original, untouched, unspoilt; and
the contrasts natural vs artificial, natural vs man-made. However,
what mattered was not these grammatical terms but whether usage
implied the definition of nature *in ways which left no legitimate place
for human use*.

In terms of strategy, arguments centred on whether the appeal
site was currently an example of virgin, untouched nature and
whether the appeal proposals would affect this status. The extract

below illustrates how the developers use this construction to argue that the appeal site is already separate from nature:

D (1): Such major features as the concrete interchange, the deep cuttings and embankments to the north and south of the interchange now dominate the local landscape. . . . These structures have already left a permanent artificial or man-made landscape; the *natural* landscape of the valley has been dramatically disturbed. (*W*)

This piece of text is interpreted as using a discourse of 'nature as wilderness' since it is the human intervention *per se* which has changed the original 'natural landscape' to an 'artificial or man-made landscape'.

The council officials alternatively use this discursive construction to argue that the site currently exists in an untouched state. They achieve this by focusing on the original landform that currently prevails:

C (1): Viewed from the City the *natural* open hill ridge line just surmounts the roof lines of the built up areas, maintaining the countryside skirt to the City. . . . it is a very simple form of folding hillside which is called the undeveloped foothills of the Haldon Ridge. . . . we are dealing with an existing, unspoilt, *natural* countryside. (*W*)

This text is interpreted as using a construction of wilderness in using the term 'natural' to refer to what the landscape was like originally.

Having argued that the appeal site is already separate from virgin nature, the essence of the developers' arguments is that the appeal site is already spoilt and as such his proposals will be of no consequence.

The council officials, having argued that the area in and surrounding the appeal site has a currently untouched, natural landform, continue this strategy by arguing that this would be changed by the appeal proposals into an artificial and unnatural landform:

C (2): It should also be noted that the scale of the operation is such that when the development is completed, a significant change in the *natural* landform will have taken place resulting in the loss of the existing dry valley feature. (*W*)

This text is clearly interpreted as using this construction of nature since it is the change of landform which is the problem of the development.

This variety of discourse, in terms of original landform, has the added advantage that good designs for landfill sites do not change the original landform but restore artificial landforms to their original, untouched form:

C (3):   Where it happened to be a large quarry, . . . a great gorging hole that had been subject to extraction for a long period of time; he might have, at least, got back to what the profile of the land was once like. But, I mean, that is a more natural thing to fill in. (V)

Nature as passive visual harmony

This second discourse located in the text was named 'nature as passive visual harmony'. Examples of this construction of nature used metaphors of 'fit', and associated concepts of harmony, totality and character. But, what was first and foremost in identifying this discourse was whether the texts implied the social relationship of an 'on-looker passively viewing the visual harmony of an area'.

In terms of strategy, arguments centred on whether or not the surrounding area to the appeal site possessed visual harmony, whether or not the appeal site *blended* with this surrounding area, and whether or not the appeal proposals would *fit* into the visual harmony.

The strategy for the council officials was to argue not only that the surrounding area possessed visual harmony, but also that the appeal site was integral to this area:

C (4):   . . . the area still possesses a rural quality and charm which provides an attractive setting to the edge of the built up area of the City. . . . the meandering nature of the Brook, the abundance of trees, the character of the buildings scattered within it and the close knit historic form of the village. (W)

C (5):   the application site makes an all important and positive contribution to the rural qualities and visual attractiveness of the area. (W)

The developers' strategy was also to accept that visual harmony existed in the surrounding area, but that the particular appeal site was separated both from surrounding area and from the category of visual harmony:

D (2): Although the development lies on the edge of the valley of the Alphin Brook, it is clearly severed from this area by the elevated A30 dual carriageway. . . . The proposals are in a locally disturbed landscape which no longer links up with the more attractive valley bottom to the north east, . . . which have varied and undulating formations, but particularly with scattered but appreciative tree cover. (W)

While the previous extracts show that the category of visual harmony is at stake, no mention has been made of the term 'nature'. And, in order to expose how these are also using constructions of nature as passive visual harmony, it is necessary to look at the arguments over the impact of the appeal proposals.

In essence, the developers argue that the impact on visual harmony will be minimal because all the tipped waste will be hidden by series of carefully designed dams (called bunds) of earth which will hide the tipped waste and *blend* into the landscape. Implicit in their argument is the visual discord which would result from sighting of the tipped waste and the visual harmony from the earth bunds:

D (3): During the period of landfilling it is acknowledged that the landfilling proposals will be visible within the landscape, but the method of bunding will conceal the unsightly tipping operations from all public viewpoints. The appearance of the bunds, which will be visible one at a time from a considerable range of views, will be difficult to discern in the landscape. (W)

The council officials alternatively argue that the appeal proposals will be evident, obvious and, by implication, unnatural. They argue this, not because they dispute that the bunds will hide the tipped waste, but because of the *visual discord* which the bunds would produce on the landscape. The specifics of the visual discord derive both from the *scale* and *form* of the proposals in relation to the existing landscape:

C (6): All his devices, to argue from his viewpoint, achieve a concealment or blend – we don't accept – they are all artificial imposed elements that are alien to the *natural* form that prevails there presently. (W)

C (7): Their configuration (re: bunds) was not particularly in sympathy with the surrounding countryside. ... Whenever you see the formation of earth bunds, it's an extremely

> long time before the harsh angularity of these construc-
> tions is faintly softened to form a sort of blend with *natural
> nature* which is invariably curved and not rectilinear. (*W*)

The two previous extracts show the term 'nature' being used to
refer to what a landscape looks like. In particular, they show natural
landscapes to be composed of features which only include human
development if they are not too big, not too angular and generally
in sympathy with the existing character and charm of the landscape.
And as texts D2, D3, C4, C5 share the same implied social relationships and grammatical forms as the extracts C6 and C7, it is
interpreted that these former extracts were also using a construction of 'nature as passive visual harmony'.

Nature as the visual harmony of activities

The third discourse located in the text was named 'nature as visual
harmony of activities'. Like the former discourse, constructions of
this discourse also included metaphors of 'fit' and concepts of
harmony, rhythm and balance. However, while grammatically similar
to the previous discourse, this discourse of nature was recognized
by the definition of nature in terms of the 'visual harmony of an
environment's activities or uses'.

In terms of strategy, arguments using this construction surrounded
whether the present activity of farming and the proposed activity
of landfilling were natural uses. The developers' main use of this
construction was to argue that the present use of the land was not
natural, while that of the council officials was to argue that the present activity was a natural use while the proposed activity was not.
In other words, as in the previous two constructions of nature, the
developers' strategy was to separate the particular appeal site from
the category of nature while the council officials' was to argue for
its centrality.

In terms of the current use of farming, the two extracts below
illustrate the difference between the developers and the council
officials:

C (8):   Many planning applications have been refused in the area
         for various reasons, notably that they were undesirable com-
         mercial intrusions into rural areas. . . . The local area forms
         a central backdrop to Exeter and is flanked by normal
         agricultural and horticultural users. (*W*)

D (4):   The area of land, around and including the appeal site, . . .
            comprises an area which is intensively farmed. (*W*)

The interpretation here is that a category distinction is being made
between those activities which are defined as 'rural', 'normal
agricultural' and 'horticultural' from activities defined as 'intensive'
and 'commercial'; and that the essence of the difference is that the
former imply irregular and small-scale human intervention, while
the latter imply regular and large-scale intervention.

The following extracts illustrate how this distinction is made
between these two forms of activities in relation to the activity of
landfilling. They show, in particular, the council officials' argument
that the landfilling proposals 'are not like agricultural practices' and
the implicit agreement by the developers:

D (5):   They (re: the proposed landfilling activities) involve
            engineering operations. I don't know whether I would
            call them substantial, but yes, they are large. (*S*)
C (9):   The site operations are not like agricultural practices, but
            more akin to road construction or quarry. (*W*)

Finally, the next extract shows how the category distinction can
be made sense of in relation to a discourse of 'nature as the visual
harmony of activities'. In particular, one set of activities rely on non-
human, seasonal forces while the other set of activities are constrained
solely by human actions and decisions:

C (10):   Vehicles coming to the site would also produce a regular
            and insensitive disturbance within the landscape which
            at present sees the passing of the seasons marked only by
            tractors and farming activities. . . . The point about the
            ploughed fields is that it is a seasonal occurrence, and your
            earthworks will be undertaken in your statement on site
            when no other vehicles will be out. (*W*)

Nature as ecological balance

The fourth and final discourse of nature located in the text was named
'nature as ecological balance'. It was identified through concepts of
harmony, diversity, sustainability and balance. However, what was
crucial for identification was for the definition of nature to be made,
not in visual terms, but in terms of *ecological impact*. The social
significance of this construction was that all human activity could

not be separated from nature as all activities have ecological consequences; albeit some more harmful and polluting than others.

Very little use was made of this construction in the inquiry as
it related to the activity of landfill. Indeed, no mention was made
by either the council officials or the developers within the public
inquiry. Use of this construction was made however, by a community group, Friends of the Earth, in their argument against the
general concept of landfill:

> Landfill should also be used at the end of the recycling line. . . .
> The long term costs of landfill are not mentioned. . . . I therefore
> oppose the landfill site proposed as it is unnecessary, environ-
> mentally damaging, and an irresponsible waste of the county's
> resources. (W)

Importantly, while these points were not made by council officials
within the public inquiry proceedings, they were made in subsequent interviews:

C (11):   So, you know, you try to look at waste in a different way;
          you try to get something out of it rather than forget it
          which is the landfill way. Because, once you have got a
          landfill site and you leave it there, there is nothing you
          can do with it . . . so, it is very much a – bury it, and
          forget about it really, and don't go back to it. (V)

The interpretation that the aforementioned passages are using a construction of nature as ecological balance lies in their critical questioning of the activity of landfill in terms of its impact on resources
and its polluting consequences (i.e. the fact that due to methane,
leachate and subsidence one cannot use a landfill site productively
for many years). The link between nature and the ecological consequences of human activity is made more explicit in the passage
below:

C (12):   The philosophy is whether you want to preserve the
          environment you have got and make best use of it, or
          whether you want to keep polluting it, willy nilly, and
          suffer the consequences in future years. . . . Whatever you
          do to the environment you have got to appreciate that
          we live in balance with *nature*. . . . *Nature* has a way of
          fighting back. (V)

Arguments using different constructions of nature

The previous section looked at four different constructions of nature and some of the arguments which occurred within each of these constructions. However, there were also texts which made use of different discourses of nature. These passages will be divided into one set of arguments which used different discourses which were both *competing* and in contradiction, and another set of texts in which it was ambiguous as to which discursive constructions were being used.

It was noted previously that while different discourses could be distinguished from each other in terms of what they implied *socially*, they also, at times, *shared similar or identical metaphors, similes, and other grammatical forms*. This possibility led to difficulties in determining which construction of nature was being used in texts. For example, the following extracts illustrate this ambiguity:

C (13): The appeal site lies within a tract of *unspoilt* and scenically attractive area of open agricultural land. (*W*)

C (14): The currently *unspoilt* nature of the application site . . . provides the rural backdrop which constitutes an invaluable visual amenity. (*W*)

In these passages, the ambiguity lies in the term 'unspoilt'. If the term 'unspoilt' referred to an untouched state this would contradict the description of the site as 'open agricultural' and 'rural', terms which imply human usage. However, if the term 'unspoilt' refers to appropriate usage (e.g. not commercial or urban) then there would be no contradiction.

However, there also existed texts where the essence of the argument related to contesting one construction of nature with another. What is interesting in these cases is how this form of analysis makes sense of what otherwise appear uninteresting and banal pieces of text.

One such piece occurred in a piece of cross-examination between the developers and a council official. The piece concerned whether the area surrounding the appeal site could be legitimately described as 'green hills':

C (15): The site contributes to the integrity of the range of green hills to the west and south-west of the City.

D (6): It depends whether you refer to the 'green hills' as a planning area of 'green hills' or as 'green hills' as I understand them.

C (16):   However, it is characterized in policy terms: the area comprises green gently undulating hills.

D (7):   They are not always green. If I may finish, I would say that the colours change as I said in my statement, so they are not always green. They are multicoloured.

C (17):   They are predominantly green, aren't they?

D (8):   Well, I accept they are predominantly green.

C (18):   And pastureland tends to remain green throughout the year, does it not?

D (9):   Pastureland does or can remain green. I suppose it can go yellow. (S)

My interpretation of this extract is that the developers and council officials are contesting the legitimacy of two discourses of nature. Specifically, the developers are contesting the official description of the area as 'green hills' which is taken for granted by the council officials. This description, using a discourse of nature as passive harmony, is deemed invalid to the developers as it does not take into account the seasonal changes that currently take place in the area. In effect, the developers are contesting this construction with a construction of nature as the visual harmony of activities; a construction which in taking into account seasonal change would be more legitimate to the changes in the landscape that would result from the landfill proposals.

DISCOURSE CONSTRUCTION, ARGUMENTATIVE PROCESS AND OUTCOME

This final section will look at the relationship between argumentative strategies used in the inquiry and in the Inspector's report — a report which in effect constituted the final outcome. It will be divided into two parts, the first looking at constraints to the argumentation in the inquiry, and the second looking at the effect of these constraints upon the outcome.

The major constraint to this inquiry concerned the existing planning legislation and its impact on what was interpreted to be legitimate argument. The specific effect of the legislation was to prioritize arguments using a construction of nature as passive harmony. This was achieved through the formal reasons given for refusal; reasons which stated:

the proposed development would be an intrusive element in the landscape and would adversely affect the visual quality of the valley ... the proposed development would be detrimental to the range of hills comprised within the Area of Great Landscape Value. (*W*)

This was interpreted as using a discourse of 'nature as passive visual harmony', since it stressed the significance of the development in '*purely visual*' terms; since it implied a *passive relationship* between viewer and landscape; and finally, since it implied the unacceptability of changes which intruded into the landscape.

However, the legitimization of this construction of nature did not negate other arguments using other constructions being used in the inquiry. What it does signify, however, is that all the arguments outlined above using the other three constructions of nature had the function, not only to contest the acceptability of the proposals, but also to *contest the grounds for accepting the proposals*. The final part will analyse the official outcome in terms of the constructions of nature used by the inspector.

In the final report the inspector chose to accept the essence of the council officials' arguments and to turn down the appeal. In judging the proposals, he predominantly used arguments using constructions of nature as passive visual harmony. The next extract shows the inspector accepting the essence of the council officials' arguments in relation to visual harmony:

I (1):   In my opinion the resulting change in the local scene would be significant and would detract from the present open rolling vista. The valley form as part of the backdrop would be lost and this part of the setting for the City would become more bland. (*W*)

However, the following extract shows the inspector also judging the impact of the proposals through a construction of nature as visual harmony of activities:

I (2):   In the shorter term the on–site activities, although partly screened, would be obvious from a number of points and while any noise would be hidden against the background of traffic, the activity level would be alien to this agricultural setting. (*W*)

The basis of this interpretation lies in the reference to the existing site in terms of the current activity of farming, and the significance of the proposed activity in terms of its 'alien activity level'. In other words, the inspector is signifying the importance of the change of activities both in terms of their quality (i.e. the fact they would be 'obvious') and in terms of their quantity (the fact that 'the activity level would be alien').

The significance of these official reasons for refusal are twofold. First, it shows how arguments using constructions of 'nature as passive visual harmony', and 'nature as visual harmony of activities' were legitimate criteria for judging the proposals; and how arguments using constructions of 'nature as wilderness' or 'nature as ecological balance' were illegitimate *vis-à-vis* their absence. Second, it showed that while the wider social and institutional factors (e.g. the current planning legislation) limited and constrained the legitimacy of available arguments, the grounds for 'what was permitted to count' were not only contested within the inquiry, but to some extent changed.

DISCUSSION

The significance of the discourse study relates both to existing research on the category of nature and to existing theory on rhetoric and discourse.

In relation to existing research on nature the discourse study is significant in its identification of four distinct discourses of nature. And, in identifying how different arguments within the public inquiry were based on quite different definitions of what nature was, the study is significant in challenging the assumption of a *pre-existing* realm of the natural.

Moreover, the discourse study is especially significant in relation to existing psychological research which currently predefines nature as *wilderness*. What the study showed was that while this construction existed and was used in arguments over the appeal site, not only did other constructions of nature exist, but it was these which were used in determining the outcome.

In particular, it was a discourse of nature as 'passive visual harmony' which was used in the interpretations of the planning policies, and that it was these along with arguments based on a construction of 'nature as harmony of activities' that determined the outcome. This finding shows that existing psychological research on nature is limited by ignoring the legitimacy of other discourses of nature.

In relation to existing theory and research on discourse and rhetoric, this study is relevant for a number of reasons. First, it is an empirical example of Billig's (1987) largely theoretical work on the process of *argumentation*. In effect, it looks at the processes of argumentation over the category of nature in terms of a struggle between conflicting processes of particularization and generalization; i.e. the relationship between the particular appeal site and the particular appeal proposals to the general category of nature.

In relation to discourse theory, the study is significant in illustrating empirically a definition of discourse in terms of its implied *social relationships*. The analysis is not only an example of this theoretical approach, but also demonstrates its practical usefulness in relating different discursive constructions to a variety of uses, human activities and outlooks these legitimate.

In relation to both rhetoric and discourse theory, this study is also significant in illustrating how the processes of argumentation both *within* and *between* different discourses of nature had very real consequences on the shape of the physical environment – e.g. a case where words really did move mountains. And finally, it illustrates how these processes of argumentation were both constrained by, and determinant of, external sources of power in a framework of social relationships. In other words, arguments over nature could not be seen as free floating but constrained and limited by existing power structures of what was permitted to count.

These points can be seen as some of the benefits of the discourse analysis. However, there were also a number of limitations relating to both the theoretical approach and the operationalization of this particular discourse analysis.

One limitation of this analysis relates to the identification of examples of usages of different discourses of nature. The difficulty lay in the fact that often texts were interpreted as using a particular construction of nature when the term 'nature' was not made explicit. And, even when a rigorous coding system was worked out there were still a number of examples where it was still unclear whether a construction of nature was being used as opposed to a construction of something else.

The basis of this difficulty lay in the dominance of a discourse of nature as wilderness. This power can be illustrated in extracts below which occured in interviews with participants of the inquiry when it was made explicit that the term 'nature' was in dispute:

D (10):   Well, you see me smiling because er, any landscape in Britain, especially in southern lowland Britain is not natural at all; it's man-made. I mean, for example, that valley had

naturally a small seasonal stream. . . . So, to say it's natural
— it's not natural. (V)

C (19):   And the question still remains: what is a natural landscape?
And we have not got natural landscapes. You know that
as well as I do. (V)

C (20):   There's very little natural vegetation left in this country;
it's all been lost — it's biologically or ecologically called
semi-natural in that it has been tampered with to a degree
by man. (V)

From these extracts it became obvious that a discourse of nature
as wilderness is singularly inappropriate as a construction to judge
the appeal proposals since: (i) it doesn't distinguish between different
types of human intervention; and (ii) the appeal site can in no way
be accurately described as wilderness. Yet, it is a wilderness construction that is deployed when it was made explicit in subsequent
interviews that the debate concerns nature. This aspect, I interpret,
led to the major difficulty in the analysis: i.e. how to unravel usages
of constructions of nature where those same arguments did not (or
indeed could not as this would be a self-defeating strategy) make
the term 'nature' explicit.

A second limitation concerned the problem of generality. While
the discourse analysis showed a *variety* of constructions of nature
used, and thereby the *availability* of the different constructions
to the participants; it leaves aside the question of how general
they are in current usage. Specifically, it leaves unanswered the question whether they are generally used across different cultures and
contexts, or whether they are more limited in use to this particular
culture and context.

And finally, it leaves aside the question of consequence. As
constructed in this analysis, a discourse becomes identified in terms
of its social implications. In other words, one discourse implies
particular sets of social relationship and uses, and another discourse
others. And implicit in this argument is the logic that different
discourses led to different consequences (e.g. different sets of power
relationships produced by different psychological consequences). Yet,
a discourse analysis as a methodology leaves unanswered the relationship between different discourses and the processes by which
they legitimate different activities, outlooks and social relationships.

To conclude, these limitations are seen, not as unresolv-
able problems arising from this discourse analysis, but as issues

brought to light via a discourse methodology. And, in order to further enquiry into our understanding of the category of nature, its different constructions and their consequences, new studies are required which will involve both the methodology of discourse analysis and its conjunction with other methods of inquiry.

REFERENCES

Billig, M. (1987) *Arguing and Thinking: A Rhetorical Approach to Social Psychology*, Cambridge: Cambridge University Press.

—— (1990) 'Psychology, rhetoric, and cognition', *History of the Human Sciences* 2 (3): 289–307.

Herzog, W. (1987) 'A cognitive analysis of preference for natural environments: mountains, canyons, and deserts', *Landscape Journal* 6: 140–52.

Ibañez, T. (1991) 'Henri, Serge . . . and the next generation', *BPS Social Psychology Section Newsletter* 24: 5–14.

Kaplan, R. (1977) 'Preference and everyday nature: method and applica tion', in D. Stokols (ed) *Perspectives on Environment and Behaviour: Theory, Research, and Applications*, New York: Plenum.

—— (1984) 'Wilderness perception and psychological benefits: an analysis of a continuing program', *Leisure Sciences* 6: 271–90.

—— (1985) 'Nature at the doorstep: residential satisfaction and the nearby environment', *Journal of Architectural and Planning Research* 2: 115–27.

Kaplan, S., Kaplan, T. and Wendt, J.S. (1972) 'Rated preference and complexity for natural and urban visual material', *Perception and Psychophysics* 12: 354–6.

Potter, J. and Wetherell, M. (1987) *Discourse and Social Psychology: beyond Attitudes and Behaviour*, London: Sage.

—— (1988) 'Accomplished attitudes: fact and fiction in racist discourse', *Text* 8: 51–68.

Potter, J.,Edwards, D., Gill, R. and Wetherell, M. (1990) 'Discourse: noun, verb or social practice?' *Philosophical Psychology* 3 (2): 205–17.

Talbot, J.F. and Kaplan, S. (1986) 'Perspectives on wilderness: re-examining the values of extended wilderness experiences', *Journal of Environmental Psychology* 6: 177–88.

Ullrich, R.S. (1983) 'Aesthetic and affective response to natural environ- ment', in I. Altman and J.F. Wohlwill (eds) *Behaviour and the Natural Environment*, New York: Plenum.

Ullrich, J.R. and Ullrich, M.F. (1976) 'A multidimensional scaling analysis of perceived similarities of rivers in western Montana', *Perceptual and Motor Skills* 43: 575–84.

Wetherell, M. (1986) 'Linguistic repertoires and literary criticism: new directions for the social psychology of gender', in S. Wilkinson (ed.) *Feminist Social Psychology*, Milton Keynes: Open University Press.

Wetherell, M. and Potter, J. (1989) 'Discourse analysis and the identification of interpretative repertoires', in C. Antaki (ed.) *Analysing Everyday Explanation: A Case Book*, London: Sage.
Wohlwill, J.F. (1983) 'The concept of nature: a psychologist's view', in I. Altman and J.F. Wohlwill (eds) *Behaviour and the Natural Environment*, New York: Plenum.

Part II

The rhetorics of politics and identity

Chapter 5

Justifying injustice: broadcasters' accounts of inequality in radio

Rosalind Gill

What I want to do in this chapter is to use the discourse analytic approach developed by Potter and Wetherell (1987) to examine broadcasters' accounts for the lack of women disc jockeys (DJs) at the radio stations where they work. It forms part of a wider project concerned with the ideological features of DJs' on-air talk and how this is understood or 'read' by radio listeners, and the ways in which DJs construct their role and their audience.

One of the most striking features of popular radio in contemporary Britain is the lack of female DJs – at least during the day. When radio stations do employ women as presenters they tend to be on in the evenings when audiences have historically and consistently been at their lowest. BBC Radio One is a good example of this: during weekday daytime programming, women are conspicuous by their absence[1] whilst a small handful have been allocated night-time or weekend slots. Such inequalities in the number and status of women DJs have been well-documented (Baehr and Ryan, 1984; Karpf, 1980, 1987).

What has been less well researched, however, is how these inequalities are understood and made sense of by people working within radio. The aim of this chapter is to examine the accounts put forward by five male DJs and programme controllers (PCs) to explain the lack of female DJs both at their own stations and more generally. In this way we should learn something about how this inequality is perpetuated.

The approach used in this chapter is one which draws, with certain reservations (see Gill, 1991) on Potter and Wetherell's formulation of discourse analysis (Potter and Wetherell, 1987; Potter et al., 1990; Edwards and Potter, 1992). This work acknowledges theoretical debts to a variety of different approaches: linguistic philosophy and speech-act theory (Austin, 1962; Searle, 1969; Wittgenstein, 1953, 1980); semiology and post-structuralism (Barthes, 1964, 1972, 1977; Derrida, 1978; de Saussure, 1974); ethnomethodology and conversation analysis (Garfinkel, 1967; Heritage, 1984; Wieder, 1974); and recent studies of rhetoric (Billig, 1987; Simons, 1989). From this disparate collection of work a coherent approach to language and discourse has been fashioned, which has been articulated primarily in relation to the sociology of scientific knowledge, and social psychology.

ANALYSING BROADCASTERS' ACCOUNTS

The analysis which follows uses a discourse analytic approach to study the accounts of five broadcasters from two independent local radio (ILR) stations for the lack of female DJs. In terms of female DJs neither station was atypical; one had no female DJs at all, whilst the other employed one female whose phone-in show was broadcast twice a week between 11.00 p.m. and 1.00 a.m. (For reasons of clarity I will treat these two stations as if they were one, which I shall call Radio Matchdale.) Two of the five broadcasters were DJs, two were programme controllers (PCs) and the fifth was both a DJ and a deputy PC. The interviews were conducted by a female interviewer and covered a range of topics including how the broadcaster saw his role and responsibilities, what he saw as the function of the station, his view of the audience, how much autonomy he felt he had, as well as questions about the lack of women DJs.[2]

What I am interested in are what Wetherell *et al.* (1987) have called the 'practical ideologies' through which gender inequalities in the employment of DJs are understood. The transcripts were analysed to find the broad types of accounts being offered by the broadcasters for the lack of women DJs. Five different types were identified, each organized around a particular claim, such as 'women don't apply' or 'the audience prefers male DJs'. What I want to stress is that these were not alternative accounts which were espoused by individual broadcasters. Rather, the DJs and PCs *all* drew on and combined different and contradictory accounts for the lack of women DJs. The analysis is divided into four sections, which deal with four of the five accounts, and examine some of the warrants which were put forward to support each broad account. The aim is not to provide an exhaustive analysis but simply to give a sense of how discourse analysis can be used to analyse this sort of material.

Accounting for inequality: (1) 'Women just don't apply'

The first and most prevalent type of account offered for the lack of female DJs was organized around the claim that women do not 'apply' to become radio presenters. Four out of the five broadcasters drew on this idea. ((.) indicates a pause in speech.)

Extract one (Goodman)
Int: Why do you think there are so few female DJs?
DJ: (laughs) probably because they don't apply. It's, it's that literally is it.

Extract two (Dale)
DJ: It's a more popular sort of occupation to men. We get a lot of tapes from people who want to be DJs and they're all from men.

Extract three (Chapman)
PC: It's a question that. I get tapes from hopefuls on my desk every day of the week and none of them are ever women.

Extract four (Lightfoot)
PC: I get all the applications to come in here (.) We get about 400 a year (.) We've had none from women in the last year. Not one to be a presenter.

One of the most interesting features of these interviews is that for each of the broad explanations put forward to explain the lack of women DJs, such as the one above that women do not apply, the broadcasters spontaneously offered further accounts, often constructed around little narratives or stories. These can be understood as ways of *warranting* their explanations which make them sound more plausible. In the case of the claim that no women apply to become DJs, four different types of supporting account can be identified – that women are not interested in becoming DJs, that 'education and social process' does not prepare them for it, that they opt instead for jobs in journalism or television, and that they are put off DJing because 'it's a man's world'. Here I will examine two of these.

Accounting for women's non-application: 'There aren't many ... who are interested in doing it'

In the following extract the PC, Chapman, has just been explaining how Radio Matchdale recruits its staff.

Extract five (Chapman)

PC: and it's where people come from (.) so in hospital radio there
      aren't many women DJs (.) there aren't many women DJs
      in pubs (.) there aren't many female DJs (.) especially teenage
      age which is when we're looking to bring people like (.) who
      are interested in doing it.

What Chapman is doing here is accounting for the lack of women
DJs at Radio Matchdale by reference to the lack of women DJs in
the station's traditional recruiting ground – hospital radio and pubs.
But he does not stop there: he offers an explanation for this – 'there
aren't many women . . . who are interested in doing it'. In making
this psychologistic claim, Chapman does two things. First, and most
straightforwardly, he denies that there is any *real* or *genuine* motivation on women's part to become DJs. It would be interesting to
discover just how common is this pattern of accounting. I want to
suggest that the idea that oppressed groups do not 'really' want to
change their position, is one frequently drawn on by members of
dominant groups in order to justify their actions or inaction.

   Second, this assertion serves to deflect criticism or charges of sexism
from radio stations in general and from Radio Matchdale in
particular. It gives the impression that radio stations would be happy
to take on women as DJs but that they are faced with a wall of
disinterest from women. The idea that radio stations are battling
against women's lack of interest in DJing, and are even putting in
extra effort to find female presenters is reinforced by Chapman's
comment a few moments later: 'so we have to look hard'. That
Chapman is looking hard for female DJs establishes his 'good faith',
his lack of sexism, and responsibility for the lack of female DJs is
placed firmly on women's shoulders.

   The idea that women are not interested in becoming DJs is also
drawn on by Goodman.

Extract six (Goodman)

DJ: I'm sure there's a helluva lot of them out there that would
      be really er good communicators but have never even given
      a thought of doing it (.) Maybe they're doing a job that either
      pays more money or is more interesting to them.

This is an explanation which rests upon an implicit view of society
as characterized by social mobility. It suggests that women *could*
become DJs but have *chosen* to do other work. The salary and

satisfaction of a radio presenter is downgraded. In fact, women's non-application is made to appear eminently sensible and rational when contrasted with the likelihood that they are doing better paid or more interesting jobs. Again, the picture presented of women doing other highly paid and satisfying work serves to undermine the notion that women *really* wish to become radio presenters.

Accounting for women's non-application: 'It's a man's world'

A different explanation for women's claimed non-application is put forward by the PC named Lightfoot.

Extract seven (Lightfoot)
PC: It's also very much a man's world so they're picked on if they
         are here (.) you know a woman has got to assert herself pretty
         definitely if she's working in radio.

It is clear that the phrase 'it's a man's world' is being used to refer to much more than the simple numerical superiority of males at the radio station, since it is used to explain the 'fact' that women are 'picked on'. What's interesting, however, is the fact that it is *not formulated as sexism*. To be 'picked on' is to be subjected to nasty and unjust behaviour, but it is the behaviour of *individuals* – something that can be highlighted by trying to imagine a formulation in which a *radio station* was deemed to 'pick on' women. The choice of this construction serves further to play down any notion of structural inequality or institutional practices.

It is significant that for the first time a feature of life within the radio station is introduced to account for women's non-application. But finally, the problem is not one for the men at the radio station, nor for the radio station as a whole to deal with, but rather it is up to each individual woman to 'assert herself pretty definitely if she's working on radio'.

Accounting for inequality: (2) audience objections: 'It's a bit strange to have a woman talking to you'

A second type of explanation for the lack of female DJs focused on the audience's expected or apparently 'proven' negative reaction to female presenters.

Extract eight (Dale)

DJ: Research has proven (.) and this is not mine but it's echoed by many surveys throughout the years (.) that people prefer to listen to a man's voice on the radio rather than a woman's voice. Women like to hear men on the radio because they're used to it (.) and it's a bit strange to have a woman talking to you. And men like hearing men on the radio (.) perhaps because they're just chauvinistic. Whatever the reasons, research has borne out this fact you know that people like to have men on the radio (.) and we just go along with the consensus of opinion. We do have women — Marie does an admirable job on the phone-in. We've got a lot of women newscasters so you know there's certainly no prejudice.

The first thing to note about this extract is that it came from Dale, (see page 77) arguing that the lack of female DJs can be explained by the fact that no women apply. Here, he constructs a different explanation for the small number of female DJs. Suddenly, the lack of female presenters looks less like the result of a lack of applications from women, and more like a deliberate policy not to employ women — because of audiences' alleged preference for men. In both formulations, it should be noted, the radio station is depicted as blameless — in the first because it is women themselves who are choosing not to apply and in the second because the radio station is merely serving its audience by giving it the presenters it wants.

Several authors have pointed out that accounts which merely appear to be describing the world are more persuasive than accounts which seem to be motivated by particular interests or psychological dispositions of the speaker (Smith, 1978; Potter and Wetherell, 1988; Edwards and Potter, 1992). Thus, one of the problems for a speaker is to accomplish the 'out-thereness' (Potter and Wetherell, 1988) of their claims. One way this is achieved by Dale in this extract is through the discursive work being done by 'research' and 'surveys'.

Audience objections: research, surveys and more research

These terms give authority to Dale's claims. In the first sentence alone Dale talks about 'research' and 'surveys' implying that these are separate rather than different words for the same thing: not only has research shown it, Dale argues, but it has also been echoed by 'many surveys'. The use of these terms and their associated vocabularies such as 'proven' lend credence and a sense of object-ivity to Dale's claims.

The terms also serve to distance Dale personally from the claim that listeners would prefer to listen to a man. It is constructed not as an aspect of his own beliefs, not an opinion, but rather something 'out there' which 'research' and 'surveys' have 'proven'. Dale's *own* role, as someone involved in the recruitment and appointment of staff, in mediating between research findings and appointment policy, is completely glossed over in his talk. The research findings which 'prove' that listeners prefer male presenters and the lack of female DJs are presented as related together in a way which is totally independent of human action.

Audience objections: a 'new sexism'?

One of the most interesting features of this extract is the striking parallel with what has become known as 'new racist' discourse (Barker, 1981). This type of discourse is characterized by the tendency to justify racist acts or legislation in non-racial terms, often drawing on other values such as equality and fairness (Billig, 1988). It is also marked by denials of prejudice, frequently accompanied by the claim that it is the liberal anti-racists who are the *real* racists (Barker, 1981; Billig, 1988). Perhaps the most straightforward type of denial takes the form of the 'disclaimer' (Hewitt and Stokes, 1975). Typically, a statement such as 'I'm not being racist' is followed by a 'but' which precedes the expression of something which could easily be heard as racist.

The widespread existence of denials of prejudice has led to some discussion of the possibility that there exists a 'cultural norm against prejudice' (Barker, 1981: Van Dijk, 1984; Reeves, 1983; Billig, 1988).

Racism is generally taken to be the prototypical example of prejudice, and indeed 'prejudice' is often used as if it were synonymous with racism. Yet, if we look back at extract eight we see that there are significant similarities with the 'new racist' discourse. The most obvious of these is the disclaimer – 'We've got a lot of women newscasters so you know (.) there's certainly no prejudice.' It does not take the classic form discussed by Hewitt and Stokes (1975) – it is retrospective rather than prospective – but the work it is doing in the extract in attempting to disclaim a prejudiced identity is the same as that identified by researchers studying racist talk. In the extract here, the disclaimer is reinforced by the contrasts which are established between men who demand male presenters because they are chauvinist and the women who do so from force of habit and the radio station where 'there's certainly no prejudice'. It is worth noting Dale's use of the notion of 'chauvinism' and contrasting it with the term 'picked on' discussed in the consideration of extract seven. It is an interesting indication of the fact that broadcasters do have access to the notion of chauvinism, which, although not politicized in the same way as 'sexism', does at least have the merit of suggesting a *pattern* to discrimination. The broadcasters use this notion only to do particular work: *not* as a characterization of the radio station's behaviour, but rather an attitude with which Radio Matchdale can be contrasted favourably.

A further notable similarity with 'new racist' discourse is to be found in Dale's claim that 'we just go along with the consensus', where Dale presents himself as a mere *victim* of *other people's* prejudice. This 'I'm not prejudiced myself but the audience wouldn't like it' type of accounting bears such a similarity to new racist talk that it suggests that the existence of a 'new sexism' might be worth investigating.

Accounting for inequality: (3) gender differences: 'Those things are not as advanced . . . as far as women are concerned as with men'

A third type of explanation for the small number of female DJs focused on women's putative lack of the *qualities* and *skills* necessary to be a DJ. The following extract from Chapman is an example of this kind of account. We will examine it in some detail.

The interviewer's question is a response to Chapman's claim (see the first section of this chapter) that none of the tapes he receives from applicants are from women.

Extract nine (Chapman)

Int: Do you think there are a set of reasons why women are put off from entering the DJ world?

PC: (. . .) Presenters have to have a number of skills. They've got to have . . . they've got to be very very dextrous (.) they've got to be very familiar with technical equipment (.) they've got to have a personality they are used to expressing and they've got to have a good knowledge of music as well as having a good personality (.) and those things are *not* as

advanced in my view as far as women are concerned as with
men. Um (.) um (.) I've got to be able to sit somebody in
a radio studio and they've got to understand what they're
doing kind of thing as well as being a good broadcaster and
women (.) in their whole background are not brought up
in that kind of environment.

Two aspects of this extract are immediately striking. First that
Chapman does not appear to be answering the question he was asked.
Instead of explaining why he thinks women are put off from
applying for DJ jobs, he appears to be providing a justification for
not employing women: 'I've got to be able to sit somebody in a radio
studio . . . .' In this respect his answer is defensive. The second is
that his opening words are extremely formal. One important
effect of Chapman's use of the passive form and of his use of a list
construction (however stumbled over) of attributes needed for radio
presentation is to give the impression that certain impersonal,
objective and, crucially, non-gendered, criteria are applied to the
selection and appointment of DJs. What Chapman is suggesting is
simply that women fail to meet these (necessary) standards.

It is worth looking at this point at the *nature* of the skills and
qualities which are formulated by Chapman as necessary for DJs.
What is striking about the list is both its inexplicitness *and* the fact
that the skills mentioned do not seem to be tied to stereotypes about
gender. DJs have got to be 'very very dextrous', 'very familiar with
technical equipment', have 'a personality they are used to expressing' and 'a good knowledge of music'. With the possible exception
of 'familiarity with technical equipment', none of these qualities
seems to fit more readily with stereotypes of masculinity than
femininity. Indeed, if anything, the qualities appear to match more
closely stereotypes of women: it is women, who, according to
stereotype, are dextrous and good at expressing themselves. The
significance of this can be highlighted by rereading the extract,
substituting 'men' for 'women'.

The point is, then, that the force of the passage derives from the
list itself rather than from the specific items which comprise it. The
only arguably stereotypical item is 'familiar with technical equipment'
which is interesting both for its vagueness and for the fact that it
suggests that potential DJs should *already* be working technical equipment. Again, this supports the impression that Chapman is accounting
for not employing women rather than for why women do not apply.

As with other explanations, Chapman spontaneously offered reasons to account for why women lacked the skills and qualities necessary for a DJ. I will examine just one of these.

Explaining gender difference: 'Education and social process'

For Chapman there seems to be nothing mysterious about why women fail to live up to the selection criteria for DJs. He accounts for it with reference to 'lay sociological explanations' (Potter and Wetherell, 1988).

PC: Those things in education and social process are *not* as advanced in my view as far as women are concerned as with men (. . .) and women (.) in their whole background are not brought up in that kind of environment.

Although the language is vague, it is clear that an explanation is being constructed around notions of the contrasting socialization and education of women and men. I am not here concerned with the 'truth' or adequacy of such an explanation but rather with what its articulation achieves for Chapman.

One of the functions of the use of this lay sociological theory for Chapman is to provide a mitigation for women's failure to meet the appointment standards for DJs. In a society where at least one strong ideological current emphasizes meritocracy and individual success, failure can easily appear as blameworthy. In this extract the lay sociological theory provides a mitigation by offering reasons or causes for women's putative failure – 'education and social process' – which make it understandable and thus less potentially blameworthy. The notions of 'education' and 'social process' are ideal for doing this kind of work since they are both extremely vague and suggest no particular agency on women's parts. Yet it should be remembered that women's 'failure' is as much Chapman's construction as the mitigation for this failure. If he characterizes women as lacking the skills and qualities to become DJs, why should he also provide a mitigation for them?

Potter and Wetherell (1988) discovered similar simultaneous constructions of blame and mitigations in Pakeha (White New Zealanders') discourse about people from the Pacific Islands living in New Zealand, and have suggested why this pattern should occur. They argue that one of the problems for speakers of producing negative claims about a group of people is that it can easily be heard as prejudice, something (as discussed in the second section of this chapter) the speaker may be anxious to avoid. One of the ways in which the hearability of this can be reduced is 'to reduce the force of the blamings being made' (Potter and Wetherell, 1988: 64). And in turn one of the ways that this can be accomplished is by the use of a mitigation. In the current example, Chapman could easily be heard as an out-and-out sexist, arguing quite simply that women are not as good as men. By providing a mitigation Chapman reduces the availability of this charge.

A second related function of Chapman's use of lay sociological theory is to emphasize the 'out-thereness' of his characterization of women. That is, his spontaneous production of an account for women's 'failure' actually *reinforces* the idea that it is because women fail to meet the selection standards that there are so few women DJs. Just as the terms 'research' and 'surveys' give the impression of facticity to claims so the sociological notions suggest that Chapman is merely describing the world as it is. Chapman's independence from the object of discussion is reinforced by the regretful tone of his next remark:

Extract ten (Chapman)
Int: Well I think that in the last say ten twenty years things have changed (.) have
PC: Yes they've changed. But they haven't changed enough.

The implication is that the world is not the way he would like it to be, but that is the way it is — regardless of his motivation.

(A contrasting explanation focusing on 'natural' gender differences and aptitudes was put forward by the DJ, Goodman. I have discussed this elsewhere (Gill, 1991).)

Accounting for inequality: (4) women's voices: too 'shrill', too 'dusky' and just plain 'wrong'

The fourth type of account put forward by the broadcasters to explain the lack of women DJs centred on women's voices. In making these claims the broadcasters placed themselves within a long tradition in British broadcasting. Women's exclusion from particular types of employment within the media on the basis that their voices are 'unsuitable' is now well-documented (Ross, 1977; Karpf, 1980; Kramarae, 1989).

As recently as the 1970s similar reasons were being offered by the BBC for their refusal to employ women as newsreaders. Mileva Ross showed how the most pervasive arguments were that women's voices were 'too high' or 'lacked authority'. In the words of Jim Black, then editor of Radio Four:

> If a woman could read the news as well as a man then she could do it. But a newsreader needs to have reliability, consistency and authority. A woman may have one or two of these things but not all three. If a woman were to read the news no one would take it seriously.
>
> (quoted in Ross, 1977)

As Ross wryly comments, did he expect us to fall about laughing or just to disbelieve it? His colleague Robin Scott was of a similar opinion. He said it was 'unnatural' for women to read the news: 'There's always bad news about and it's much easier for a man to deal with that kind of material' (quoted in Ross, 1977).

The concerted efforts of the feminist campaigning group, Women In Media, led to a small handful of women being appointed as newsreaders by 1975. Jim Black spoke of 'an awful lot of special training' which had 'come to fruition' leaving two female newsreaders to take their place alongside their fifteen male colleagues. Black commented: 'I think we have got the right mix now. I don't want Radio Four to sound all-female ... If you have two on it sounds a lot' (quoted in Ross, 1977).

All the DJs and PCs interviewed in this research found women's voices worthy of comment. Although one remark by Toller seems to be a positive one – he says that he does not think the Radio Two presenter Gloria Hunniford has a shrill voice – the mere fact that he felt it worthy of comment is significant. There were no comparable remarks about men's voices. Next, we examine the rather more lengthy comments of Goodman when asked to elaborate upon his claim that women's voices are 'not right'.

Extract eleven (Goodman)

DJ: As I said to you before (.) people are sensitive to voice (.) they pick up a lot in a voice. They can see it as exuding friendliness, sarcasm, angriness or whatever and if it happens to be(.) and if a woman's voice sounds grating or high (.) shrill, then that will switch them off. If it sounds dusky and sexy (1.0) unfortunately that switches them on (.) now Marie has

got a dusky, sexy, deep voice perfect for it (.) she's actually
nothing like that when you meet her (.) she's a very sweet
lady but she's not like that but people are conned totally by
the voice.

The extract is similar to that discussed in the second section of this
chapter in that Goodman is involved in justifying not employing
women as DJs by reference to what listeners like or dislike. However,
whereas on p. 80 the listeners' resistance to female DJs was
characterized as 'chauvinist' or merely habitual, and the DJ presented
himself as regretfully just 'going along with the consensus', here
listeners' putative reservations about (some) female voices are
characterized as perfectly reasonable. What could be heard as
prejudice is recast as 'sensitivity'. Listeners' sensitivity, unlike their
chauvinism, is not to be regretted. The radio station merely translates
this sensitivity into appointment decisions.

One of the ways in which listeners' sensitivity to women's voices
is brought off as reasonable by Goodman is through the subtle
linking of notions of sensitivity to particular emotional or motiva-
tional states (angriness, friendliness, sarcasm) and sensitivity to
particular vocal pitches. Goodman starts by asserting that people see
voices as 'exuding friendliness, sarcasm, angriness or whatever' and
goes on 'and if a woman's voice sounds grating or high (.) shrill
then that will switch them off'. The 'reasonableness' of this second
phrase is effectively achieved by its ostensible connection to the first.
For whilst sensitivity to friendliness or sarcasm seems admirable,
'sensitivity' to pitch may betoken prejudice.

It is worth briefly considering the way that pairs of words are
used to characterize women's voices. The first thing to note is that
the notion of what is 'shrill' or 'dusky' is not unproblematic: these
are not neutral words to describe pitch — whatever a neutral word
may be. Indeed, Goodman starts by characterizing some women's
voices as 'high' but then substitutes a word which has far more richly
negative connotations — shrill. To object to (or be 'sensitive' to)
'high' voices could be heard as blameworthy, but to object to 'shrill'
voices seems perfectly reasonable — it is a word which contains an
evaluation (cf. Wowk, 1984).

Second, we should note the way the second word in each pair
is used to add to and to describe the first — giving the impression
that, for example, dusky *is* sexy. I want to argue that it is not
insignificant that the two examples used seem to fit almost perfectly

with two commonly used stereotypes of women – the 'nag' and the 'femme fatale'. This is not to imply, however, that these stereotypes are somehow static and non-changing.

What Goodman seems to be doing is presenting a 'no-win' situation for women. If they sound 'grating and shrill' then that 'switches listeners off'. This phrase has a fascinating double meaning. Goodman may mean simply that shrill or grating female voices displease people, turn them off. But his phrase also serves to remove all agency and responsibility for switching the radio off from listeners, and places it instead on women's voices. In this way people's sensitivity comes to seem perfectly reasonable; it is women's voices in themselves that do the switching off, and are therefore blameworthy.

If a woman sounds 'dusky and sexy' 'that switches them on'. One might imagine that this is exactly what the radio station would want, but Goodman treats it ambivalently describing it as 'unfortunate', but also describing Marie's 'dusky sexy deep' voice as 'perfect for it'. This becomes explicable if we understand the 'it' for which Marie is apparently 'perfect' as her own show (which is broadcast between 11 p.m. and 1 a.m.) rather than more prime-time radio presentation. It also illuminates a further nuance of meaning for the word 'dusky' – suggesting appropriateness for nighttime broadcasting. More generally, it seems that Goodman's ambivalence about 'switching them on' is due to its sexual connotations. This would denote a level of sexual assertiveness deemed unacceptable in a woman.

Goodman's remarks about Marie are also interesting for three other reasons. At one level they serve simply as a reminder (in what may be for the speaker a critical interpretative context) that the radio station *does have* a female presenter (albeit only one who is relegated to the wee small hours). By explicitly praising Marie's presentation style, Goodman reduces the hearability of sexism. This also accounts for his ambivalence: for he is both justifying the non-employment of women as DJs *and* attending to the possibility that he may be heard as sexist.

Second, the passage is interesting because it supports the idea raised earlier that 'dusky' and 'sexy' are tied to the notion of the 'femme fatale'. What Goodman seems to be saying is that she *sounds* dusky and sexy, but *actually* she is not – she is no 'femme fatale'.

Finally, the passage is significant because it reasserts the importance of voice – 'people are conned by the voice totally'. However, it does so in such a way as to undermine completely Goodman's earlier claim that people are 'sensitive to voices' and can 'pick up a lot in a voice'. For listeners so easily 'conned' the notion of 'sensitivity' as a justification for not employing women who apply begins to look a little thin.

It is tempting to suggest that the only way a woman can succeed is by sounding like a man. And indeed, this is what Goodman seems to have concluded.

Extract twelve (Goodman)

DJ: They they build a mental picture so it's really your voice (.) if your voice is right. For some women that can be hard because their voice is naturally higher.

If we leave aside the considerable debate over the supposed differences in the pitch of male and female voices (see, for example, Spender, 1985) what is clear from this short extract is that the male voice is being used as the norm against which other voices are judged for their appropriateness. Implicit in the extract is the idea that a low, male voice is somehow naturally right for DJs. This extract is a very good example of what has been called the 'male as norm' phenomenon (Spender, 1985; Griffin, 1985) and it is against the background of this norm that becoming a DJ can be judged 'hard' for 'some women'. Significantly, although the male voice is presented as the 'natural' 'right' voice for a DJ it is presented as non-gendered.

DISCUSSION

This chapter has examined some of the practical ideologies through which the lack of female DJs is explained and justified. What I have tried to show is that far from the broadcasters each espousing a particular attitude or advancing a specific explanation to account for the lack of women DJs, each had available a *whole range* of ways of accounting, which they drew on selectively in the interviews.

Overall, I pointed to a pervasive variability in broadcasters' accounts which would be overlooked or suppressed by more traditional, social psychological approaches. The accounts constructed by broadcasters were flexible, inconsistent and sometimes contradictory. The claim by the DJs and PCs that no women apply, within moments of explanations by those same broadcasters about why those women who do apply are not suitable for DJing, is simply the most dramatic example of this, and poses severe problems for attitude theories and all other approaches which work with a realist view of language. Rather than seeing such assertions as unproblematic statements of fact, discourse analysis argues that they are better understood in terms of their discursive functions.

The chapter also looked in detail at the construction of particular accounts, examining how broadcasters attempted to accomplish them as factual or 'out-there' and discussing the way the accounts offered seemed to make the lack of women flow apparently self-evidently from the explanations. Specifically, all the accounts put forward by broadcasters to explain the lack of women DJs constructed the reasons as lying *in women themselves* or in *the wants of the audience*. The role of the radio station was made invisible in these accounts, and discussions of employment practices and institutional sexism were conspicuous by their absence. In this way broadcasters were able to present themselves as non-sexist, whilst they simultaneously justified the lack of women at the radio station.

None of the DJs or PCs said at any point that they did not think that women should be employed as DJs. On the contrary, they were keen to point out their lack of sexism ('there's certainly no prejudice') and that they were 'looking hard' for female presenters. However, what they produced were accounts which justified the exclusion of women. In providing these accounts for why there are so few female DJs now, the broadcasters also provided justifications for the continued absence of women in the future. The ideological effects of these discourses is to perpetuate inequality within radio stations.

One potential disadvantage with this kind of discourse analytic approach is that it does not produce the broad empirical generalizations which are developed in more traditional sociological and social psychological work. Thus, the analysis here cannot be understood as identifying a universal process underlying gender discrimination in employment or even sexism in radio stations. What it does is examine the explanations put forward by a particular group of white, male broadcasters in a particular social and historical context, in the course of interviews with a white, middle-class and almost-certainly-feminist (from the broadcasters' perspective) woman. For discourse analysis, the failure to theorize universal processes is not a weakness but an inevitable consequence of the fact that explanations are always constructed out of particular interpretative resources and designed for specific occasions (Wetherell and Potter, 1988). Thus, we might expect to see different accounts put forward to explain the lack of women DJs if the broadcasters had been talking amongst themselves or had been interviewed by a male. This does not invalidate the research but merely serves to emphasize discourse analysts' point about the constructive, action-orientated nature of language.

A further disadvantage for people thinking about doing discourse analytic work is the sheer effort involved. Discourse analysis is extremely labour-intensive, and the time taken up conducting interviews and transcribing them can be considerable. In order to produce this analysis, for example, I produced five transcripts which totalled 114 pages of typed A4 script. Added to this is the length of time it takes to learn and develop the skill of analysis. As Wetherell and Potter (1988) have argued, discourse analysis is a craft skill, and it is possible to work with an analytic schema for several days only to find that it cannot be validated by the available materials.

However, against this, discourse analysis has considerable value. It offers both a practical and theoretically coherent way of analysing a whole variety of talk and texts, taking them seriously in their own right (not as vehicles for some underlying psychological reality) and treating them in their full specificity.

Discourse analysis also constitutes a *systematic* approach to the evaluation of texts whose findings are open to evaluation. Reports of discourse analytic work include either full transcripts or samples of the analytic materials used so that readers are able to assess the success of the interpretations, and indeed, offer alternatives (Wetherell and Potter, 1988).

Finally, and most importantly, discourse analysis offers a new way of understanding ideology. It sees ideological discourse not as a fixed subset of all discourse which works in standard recurrent ways and is defined by its content or style, but rather as a *way of accounting*. It highlights the fact that what is ideological cannot be straightforwardly read off: propositions do not come with their ideological significance 'inscribed on their backs' and nor is the operation of ideology limited to discourse which naturalizes, reifies or legitimizes – or any of the other familiar modes (Thompson, 1988). Discourse analysis suggests that what is ideological is an *analytic question*. In the present analysis I hope to have shown that even as broadcasters declared their desire to see more women DJs, they produced discourse which was ideological – because the accounts they produced served to justify and perpetuate inequality within radio stations.[3]

NOTES

1 Except in the new 'weathergirl' (sic) role in which female news or weather readers or production assistants are used by male DJs to feed them witty one-liners and create an impression of relaxed banter.
2 I would like to thank Sue Reilly for her help in carrying out these interviews.
3 I would like to thank Michael Billig, Jonathan Potter and Andy Pratt for their comments on an earlier draft of this chapter.

REFERENCES

Austin, J.L. (1962) *How to do Things with Words*, Oxford: Clarendon Press.
Baehr, H. and Ryan, M. (1984) *Shut Up and Listen: Women and Local Radio: A View from the Inside*, London: Comedia.
Barker, M. (1981) *The New Racism*, London: Junction Books.
Barthes, R. (1964) *Elements of Semiology*, New York: Hill & Wang.
—— (1972) *Mythologies*, London: Paladin.
—— (1977) *Image-Music-Text*, London: Fontana.
Billig, M. (1987) *Arguing and Thinking: A Rhetorical Approach to Social Psychology*, Cambridge; Cambridge University Press.
—— (1988) 'The notion of "prejudice": some rhetorical and ideological aspects', *Text* 8: 91–110.
Coward, R. (1984) *Female Desire: Women's Sexuality Today*, London: Paladin.
Derrida, J. (1978) *Writing and Difference*, London: Routledge & Kegan Paul.
De Saussure, F. (1974) *Courses in General Linguistics*, London: Fontana.
Edwards, D. and Potter, J. (1992) *Discursive Psychology*, London: Sage.
Garfinkel, H. (1967) *Studies in Ethnomethodology*, Englewood Cliffs, NJ: Prentice Hall.
Gill, R. (1991) 'Ideology and popular radio: a discourse analytic examination of disc jockeys' talk', unpublished PhD thesis, Loughborough University.
Griffin, C. (1985) *Typical Girls: Young Women from School to the Job Market*, London: Routledge & Kegan Paul.
Heritage, J. (1984) *Garfinkel and Ethnomethodology*, Cambridge: Polity Press.
Hewitt, J.P. and Stokes, R. (1975) 'Disclaimers', *American Sociological Review* 40: 1–11.
Karpf, A. (1980) 'Women and Radio', *Women's Studies International Quarterly* 3: 41–54.
—— (1987) 'Radio Times; private women and public men', in K. Davies, J. Dickey and T. Stratford (eds) *Out of Focus: Writings on Women and the Media*, London: The Women's Press.
Kramarae, C. (1989) *Technology and Women's Voices*, London: Sage.
Potter, J. and Wetherell, M. (1987) *Discourse and Social Psychology: Beyond Attitudes and Behaviour*, London: Sage.

—— (1988) 'Accomplishing attitudes: fact and evaluation in racist discourse', *Text* 8: 51–68.

Potter, J., Wetherell, M., Gill, R. and Edwards, D. (1990) 'Discourse analysis: noun, verb or social practice', *Philosophical Psychology* 3: 205–17.

Reeves, W. (1983) *British Racial Discourse: A Study of British Political Discourse about Race and Race-related Matters*, Cambridge: Cambridge University Press.

Ross, M. (1977) 'Radio', in M. Stott and J. King (eds) *Is This your Life? Images of Women in the Mass Media*, London: Virago.

Searle, J.R. (1969) *Speech Acts*, Cambridge: Cambridge University Press.

Simons, H. (1989) *Rhetoric in the Human Sciences*, London: Sage.

Smith, D. (1978) 'K is mentally ill: the anatomy of a factual account', *Sociology* 12: 23–53.

Spender, D. (1985) *Man Made Language*, London: Routledge.

Thompson, J. (1984) *Studies in the Theory of Ideology*, Cambridge: Polity.

Van Dijk, T. (1984) *Prejudice in Discourse: An Analysis of Ethnic Prejudices in Cognition and Conversation*, Amsterdam: John Benjamins.

Wetherell, M. and Potter, J. (1988) 'Discourse analysis and the identification of interpretative repertoires', in C. Antaki (ed.) *Analysing Everyday Explanation: A Casebook of Methods*, London: Sage.

Wetherell, M., Stiven, H. and Potter, J. (1987) 'Unequal egalitarianism: a preliminary study of discourses concerning gender and employment opportunities', *British Journal of Social Psychology* 26: 59–71.

Wieder, L. (1974) 'Telling the code', in R. Turner (ed.) *Ethnomethodology*, Harmondsworth: Penguin.

Wittgenstein, L. (1953) *Philosophical Investigations*, Oxford: Blackwell.

—— (1980) *Remarks on the Philosophy of Psychology*, Oxford, Blackwell.

Wowk, M. (1984) 'Blame allocation, sex and gender in a murder investigation', in *Women's Studies International Forum* 7: 75–82.

Chapter 6

Autobiography and change: rhetoric and authenticity of 'Gothic' style

Sue Widdicombe

> a teenager's desire to identify with a tribe — and to follow
> religiously its dress code — is entirely normal.
>
> *(Today* 7 July 1990)

In this chapter, I shall address two related issues: first is the issue
of why some young people join subcultures; the second is that of
the significance or meaning of subcultural style. Two sorts of answers
to these questions have been given: one sociological and the other
social psychological. I shall outline each of these briefly before
turning to a discourse analysis approach to these issues.

TWO READINGS OF YOUTH SUBCULTURES AND STYLE

The sociological accounts of youth subcultures which proliferated
in the late 1970s and early 1980s were concerned with the socio-
structural conditions and class contradictions that created problems
for male, white, working-class youth. Subcultural style was interpreted as a collective response to these shared problems because it
represented a form of symbolic resistance to dominant (middle–class)
cultural values whilst defending or reclaiming traditional working-
class values. The challenge was symbolic because it did not constitute
an actual or successful solution to subordination. From this perspective, joining a subculture can be regarded as a solution to sociostruc-
tural problems (see Brake, 1985; Hall and Jefferson, 1976; Hebdige,
1979).

The emphasis in the social psychological perspective is on
identity and its benefits for individuals. Within this approach, it is
assumed that subcultures provide a pool of available resources

which particular individuals or groups can draw upon in their attempt to make sense of their own specific situation and construct a viable identity (Brake, 1985; Murdock, 1974). The need for a viable identity is particularly acute during adolescence because physical, relational and social changes during this period, together with widening social and political interests, disturb the previously established 'self-system' or the system of categories which are used to define the self (Palmonari et al., 1984). That is, there is a need to redefine 'who I am'.

The process of joining a group is conceptualized as one of cognitive self-definition through the internalization of, in this case, a subcultural category. The result of this process is that 'the group is cognitively represented within the mind of the individual member' (Turner et al., 1987: 101). Once self-defined, individuals are said to employ a process of self-stereotyping through which they adopt criterial attributes of that category (cf. Turner, 1982; Turner et al., 1987). According to this perspective, the local 'visibility' of a particular subculture will be an important factor in joining, since others may provide models or exert influence over the individual in their decision to join (cf. Widdicombe, 1988).

Both these accounts, however, overlook the important issue of how members themselves account for the significance and meaning of the subculture, its style, and their membership. In the sociological account, the meaning of subcultures and style is regarded as a 'hidden code' which can be recovered through semiotic and structural analysis, drawing upon the conceptual tools of Marxism, Lévi-Strauss, Barthes and Althusser (Cohen, 1980).[1] Within the social psychological account, style is regarded merely as signifying membership and identity; the meaning of social identities is rarely addressed explicitly (cf. Condor, 1989). This is partly because the more interesting questions from this perspective are to do with the process of joining and the behavioural and cognitive consequences of membership on those occasions when it is salient to the individuals concerned. These processes are investigated experimentally or through the statistical analysis of questionnaire or interview responses according to theoretically derived hypotheses. Nevertheless, '[t]he nagging sense here is that these lives, selves and identities do not always coincide with what they are supposed to stand for' (Cohen, 1980: xviii).

A THIRD APPROACH: DISCOURSE ANALYSIS

The discourse analysis approach I adopt involves asking questions that differ from those outlined earlier because the focus is different: the site of investigation here is not the social structure, style, nor the individual, but language. It therefore entails collecting accounts by talking to people or generating a pool of, say, media articles about subcultures. The question, 'Why do some young people join subcultures?' is replaced in my research by a concern with autobiographical accounts of change to unconventional appearance. Instead of asking what (cognitive) processes underlie membership and its adoption, I am concerned with how the significance of change is constituted within accounts, and with what effects. I am also concerned with how the meaning of style is negotiated within the context of these accounts.

The discourse analysis approach is concerned with different issues because its assumptions differ from those more usually adopted. Traditionally, talk is *about* experiences, identities and mental states; and language is regarded merely as a tool for gaining access to this underlying reality. By contrast, the discourse analysis perspective assumes that experiences, selves and social and psychological phenomena are constituted in and through language; and that their meanings are inseparable from the ways they are described within the interactional context (Garfinkel, 1967; Potter and Wetherell, 1987: see also Gergen and Davis, 1985; Shotter and Gergen, 1989). Thus, it is assumed that lives, selves and experiences and their significance are constructed through culturally available resources and practices.

These cultural or linguistic resources are regarded as sets of shared meanings, statements, ideas, and so on which may contain contrary themes. An important point is that these cultural resources are not pre-given, fixed or finite and they can only be understood in and through their use, that is, in practice. The term 'practice' is appropriate because it indicates that language is a form of social activity; utterances do things and language or talk thus has an essential action-orientation (cf. Austin, 1962; Sacks lectures, 1964–1972; Wittgenstein, 1953). Moreover, the term suggests some form of social organization and it is assumed that talk is socially organized in at least two ways. First, it is sequentially organized (Atkinson and Heritage, 1984) and the sequential unfolding of descriptions is often significant for our understanding of what is said. Second, talk is

organized according to culturally available but tacit 'reasoning procedures' which seem to inform speakers' use of resources such as specific
words, phrases or illustrative examples. That is, utterances seem to
display a sensitivity to the kinds of inferences that are thereby made
available, and others that are thereby avoided. Often, therefore,
considering what is not said but could be said can be useful as a
preliminary step in the analysis. It is important to stress, since the
terminology is potentially confusing, that these 'reasoning procedures'
are not located in people's heads as underlying cognitive or information processes. They are, instead, dynamic and pragmatic aspects of
language use.[2]

ANALYSIS

Strategies

There are two features of the analytic strategy I adopt. First, is simply
developing a sensitivity to the way in which language is used.
Schenkein (1978) refers to this as a certain 'analytic mentality' in
so far as it involves the employment of a range of intuitive skills
and a way of looking at materials. Although these skills are tacit and
do not lend themselves to procedural description, they are not
mysterious and can be developed through practice and example (see
Wooffitt, 1990; Wootton, 1989 for more detailed discussion). The
second feature relates to the inferential and interactional aspects of
talk. Following Paul Drew (1987), I find it useful to regard the ways
things are said as a solution to a problem. The analyst's task is therefore
to identify the problem and how what is said constitutes a solution.
In other words, the analyst can examine the materials with a view
to answering three (related) questions: What interactional business
is being attended to? How do speakers demonstrate their orientation to this business? What strategies and procedures seem to inform
this orientation? (cf. Wooffitt, 1990).
      To summarize, the object of analysis is to explicate the culturally
available resources and tacit reasoning procedures which seem to
inform what is said, and to identify the nature of the interactional
tasks thereby addressed.

Background

To illustrate this approach I shall present and analyse two extracts from autobiographical accounts given by Tony and Lisa whose appearance could be classified as 'gothic': black clothes, leather jackets, dramatic eye make-up and long black hair. These extracts are taken from one of a series of discussions conducted with people who 'looked different' in various locations in London and Reading Rock Festival during September 1989 by Rob Wooffitt and myself. The discussions were recorded and subsequently transcribed verbatim.

In these extracts, Tony and Lisa describe the period in their lives when they began to change from a 'conventional' to an unconventional appearance. I will argue that the ways that their descriptions are formulated addresses a very sensitive issue. In describing change to unconventional appearance, hearers are likely to draw inferences as to what motivated that change. One obvious inference is that speakers were copying others or deliberately conforming to a particular image. This inference is perhaps especially likely given two features of their description; change took place during adolescence and it was unconventional in nature. Such reasons or motivation for change might be regarded as problematic, however, in so far as they can be used to index the shallowness of that change.

The object of this analysis is to furnish an appreciation of the ways in which the speakers orient to and negotiate this problem. Specifically, I shall identify three types of resources which are used. They concern: negotiating the existence and potential influence of others; descriptions of these potentially relevant others: and the ways that appearance is characterized as an expression of the true self.

Negotiating the existence and potential influence of others

In the following extract Tony and Lisa discuss the origins of their change to unconventional clothing ((.) indicates a pause in speech)

(Ex. 1) [1989; 14: p. 1] 17A:3G:2M/F

```
1 Sue:    was there a time when you wore conventional
2         clothing (.) or high street fashions?
3 Tony:   when I was about um up till about the age of
4         fifteen I just wore conventional clothes but I
5         didn't listen to conventional music
6 Lisa:   yeah I wore I wore my I sort of started wearing
7         like unconventional clothes when I was about
8         thirteen and like it took me a whole hour to put
9         this long black skirt on and walk down the street
```

10	see what I mean it took me a long time That's
11	when I started. I didn't know anybody else
12	dressed in black or anything I just did it purely
13	for myself

(a few lines omitted)

14 *Lisa:*	*I didn't know anybody at all. I came from a*
15	really tiny sort of really small little village
16	and like everything I did came under close
17	scrutiny. It wasn't until I was about fifteen
18	that I realized there was like loads of other
19	people who sort of dressed the same way as I did
20	or sort of the same ways things like that
21 *Tony:*	yeah cos I sort of started wearing make up and I
22	didn't even know about other people wearing it. I
23	started wearing it and putting on these black
24	clothes and things like that and then I went into
25	town one week cos like I was considered really
26	freaky by everybody. All these people who lived
27	on this estate hadn't ever seen anybody like me
28	before. I went to this town one evening and
29	walked by this pub and I saw loads of people with
30	like hair spiked up and things like that and they
31	were a lot more way out than me even though I was
32	considered the biggest freak of the area but they
33	were a lot more way out than me. I was overawed
34	by the fact that there was other people who
35	actually dressed differently to what everybody
36	else wears round the area

Tony and Lisa both identify a point in their lives when they began to change their appearance in unconventional ways, and they describe the nature of change. Their accounts, however, entail more than just a description of these changes; the speakers also refer directly and indirectly to the existence of others similarly dressed.

First, accounts of the 'what' and 'when' of change are formulated in the context of denying knowledge of others similarly attired, although this latter information is not directly relevant to the question. Thus, Lisa states that she 'started wearing like unconventional clothes when I was about thirteen . . . I didn't know anybody else dressed in black or anything' (lines 6–12). Similarly, Tony says that 'I sort of started wearing make up and I didn't even know about other people wearing it . . .' (lines 21–2). As I said earlier, when young people describe change to an unconventional appearance, hearers may draw negative inferences regarding the reasons for that change. For example, they may infer that the speakers were copying or influenced by others, or conforming to a particular image. In order for such inferences to constitute a legitimate reason for change, however, one needs to have some knowledge of the existence of unconventional others, and of the attributes that render them unconventional. Formulating change in the context of denying knowledge of potentially relevant others thus has three effects: (i) it directly denies the likely assumption that Tony and Lisa changed their appearance to conform to a particular image; (ii) it acknowledges the existence of potentially relevant others; (iii) it implicitly acknowledges that their existence could, in other circumstances, provide a reasonable explanation for change.

Second, both Tony and Lisa provide an account of an occasion on which they became aware of the existence of potentially relevant others. These accounts clearly establish the temporal order of events; the origins of change occurred prior to the discovery of similarly alternative others, even though these others did exist at the time. Lisa, for example, states that she began changing her appearance at about the age of thirteen although 'it wasn't until I was about fifteen that I realized there was like loads of other people who sort of dressed the same way as I did' (lines 17–19). Tony states that he started changing his appearance and *then* he 'went to this town one evening and walked by this pub and saw loads of people with like hair spiked up . . .' (lines 28–30). His reaction to this discovery further confirms the temporal order in so far as he was '*overawed* by the fact that there was other people who actually dressed differently . . .' (lines 33–5). In addition, it is through these descriptions that speakers are able to account for their current knowledge of the existence of similarly alternative others whilst simultaneously warranting their denial that it can be used to explain their own change to unconventional appearance.

Third, both speakers refer to the locale in which they grew up and in which change took place. First, Lisa describes the difficulty she experienced in presenting herself publicly in her 'long black skirt'. She says: 'It took me a whole hour to [put the skirt on] and walk down the street . . . it took me a long time' (lines 8–10). Since the action of putting on a skirt does not normally take a 'whole hour', and since the action of walking down the street in an article of clothing is not in itself difficult, we can infer that the difficulty lies in the anticipation of others' reactions. This difficulty is rendered more comprehensible in the context of Lisa's next reference to the locale. She says that 'I came from a really tiny sort of really small little village and like everything I did came under close scrutiny' (lines 14–17). This description portrays an image of a small community in which everyone knows everyone else and is interested in and knowledgeable about their business (hence 'everything I did came under close scrutiny'). Such places are not normally associated with trend-setting or style consciousness, and neither do they tend to have the retail outlets to support alternative style. Moreover, the strong sense of community and scrutiny gives the impression of a place in which conformity is rife; where, moreover, pressures to conform would normally tend to sanction against nonconformity. Lisa's description of her immediate locale at the time of change therefore further warrants her claim that there were no models around to influence her.

Tony refers to the inhabitants of the estate on which he lived at the time of change. He says that 'I was considered really freaky by everybody. All these people who lived on this estate hadn't ever seen anybody like me before' (lines 25–8). The first point to notice about this utterance is its sequential position in the account. That is, its insertion between two beginnings of his description of how he came to realize that there were others ('I went to this town . . .' on lines 24–5 and line 28), indicates its significance for that story. The second point is that Tony's difference is described from the perspective of the estate dwellers: they considered him 'freaky' (because) they had not seen anyone like him before. The third point is that in his description of their reaction to his appearance, Tony uses the extreme case formulations, '*everybody*' and '*ever* seen *anybody* like me before'. These formulations make the strongest possible case for, and hence justify, the claim with which they are associated (Pomerantz, 1986). Drawing upon these observations, one effect of characterizing their reaction as he does is to indicate their (and by implication his own) naivety as regards the existence of nonconformist others and the absence of such others in the vicinity. It hence provides the relevant background to his later account in so far as it emphasizes that their existence was something he had to discover. The use of extreme case formulations clearly legitimates his denial of knowledge of potentially influential others.

To summarize, in describing the origins of change to unconventional appearance, Tony and Lisa are faced with a problem: the existence of alternative others could warrant the assumption that change was in some way influenced by or because of them. They negotiate this problem by suggesting that, whilst the presence of others might provide an adequate explanation for change in other circumstances, it is not appropriate in their cases. They do so by indicating their lack of awareness of potentially relevant others in three ways: through an explicit denial of such knowledge; through providing an account of how they later came to realize the existence of these others; and through their description of the 'naivety' of the locale in which change took place. The credibility of their accounts is further enhanced by the ways in which the potentially influential others are described.

The nature of the relevant others

In the extract above, Tony makes three references to 'unconventional' and hence potentially relevant others. First, he says that at the time he began changing his appearance, he was not aware of others (men) who wore make-up. He later describes an observation of a group of people whose appearance made him realize the existence of similarly unconventional others. He says that he saw 'loads of people with like hair spiked up and things like that' (lines 29–30). There is an interesting but implicit contrast between those features of his own and of others' appearance that suggest nonconformity. Their nonconformity is indicated by their hairstyle, his by wearing make-up; moreover, he describes wearing black clothes and 'things like that', but makes no direct reference to the others' clothing.

Tony's second reference to the others is made in the context of a direct comparison between his own appearance and theirs: 'they were a lot more way out than me' (lines 32–3). He thus suggests that whilst the others are also unconventional, there is a difference in the degree to which he and they are unconventional.

Tony's third reference to potentially relevant others occurs when he describes his reaction to the discovery that others also ascribed to an unconventional appearance. He states that 'I was overawed by the fact that there was other people who actually dressed differently to what everybody else wears round the area' (lines 33–6). An alternative, more succinct, and equally plausible way of formulating his reaction might be that 'I was overawed by the fact that there were other people who also dressed differently'. Such a description would flow more directly from his previous comparison between his and their 'freakiness'. Instead, however, Tony compares their appearance with 'what everybody else wears round the area'.

The point is that each reference to these unconventional others avoids focusing upon or emphasizing similarity between his own appearance and theirs. That is, the first reference to the others implies that any similarity between himself and these others lies in the fact that they appear unconventional, and not in the nature of that unconventionality. His second reference limits or undermines the extent of the similarity between himself and the others entailed by nonconformity. Finally, the reference to 'what everybody else wears' establishes a standard or norm according to which they deviate. The implication is that he also deviates, but not necessarily in the same way. It is proposed that Tony's references to alternative others displays a sensitivity to the potential reaction of disbelief to a high degree of coincidence: for if what he discovered were people who dressed exactly the same as himself, the credibility of his earlier denial of knowledge of similar others, and hence the absence of influence, would have been undermined. Lisa similarly appears to display such sensitivity when she corrects her initial statement that she realized there were 'other people who sort of dressed *the same way*' (line 19) to one that is more vague and therefore makes available less strong inferences as to the degree of similarity: 'sort of the same ways things like that' (line 20).

There is a further point. In denying knowledge of similarly dressed others, speakers refer to collections of others or 'loads of people' whose appearance is characterized by black clothes, spiked-up hair and so on. The features that the speakers describe make available, in this context, particular category labels or terms; namely, goths or punks (cf. Sacks, 1972). Building upon this observation, it seems that speakers' avoidance of the inference that they were conforming to a particular image could be accomplished in a more straightforward manner by denying explicitly that they were aware of the existence of punk or gothic subcultures. It is interesting therefore that they do not employ such labels.

Wooffitt (1992) suggests that being able to name some state of affairs or an object implies having knowledge about them, such that one can recognize what counts as that object or state of affairs. Moreover, naming suggests a commitment to the in-principle existence of the object so named, and can be taken as an indication of interest in the phenomenon. Drawing upon these observations, had Tony or Lisa named the relevant others as gothics or punks, we might infer that they were able at the time to recognize these others as members and thus that they had the appropriate criterial knowledge of what counts as gothic or punk. We might, moreover, infer some interest in those subcultures. The availability of such inferences would, however, undermine their implicit claim that they were not motivated by a desire to conform to a particular image at the time.

To summarize, both speakers describe an encounter with similarly non-conventional others. In describing these others they display a sensitivity to the kind of incredulous reaction that might greet the coincidence of sameness or their ability to name these others as, say, gothic. Moreover, that the others are not named deflects the inference that change has to do with more than appearance; that, in other words, it might have something to do with their interest in subcultural forms.

Appearance as an expression of true self

I have suggested that descriptions of change to unconventional appearance are designed to avoid the inference that change was motivated by a desire to copy others or to conform to a particular image. A third means of avoiding these negative inferences is the provision of an alternative reason for changing appearance. In extract (1) (pages 98–9), Lisa says 'I just did it purely for myself' (lines 12–13). In the following extract, which occurs a few lines later in the inter-view transcript, Tony also provides a reason for change. He does so in the context of responding to my request for an autobiographical account of change.

(Ex. 2) [1989; 14: p. 2] 17A:3G:2M/F

1 *Tony*:	I mean ever since I started wearing clothes which I
2	chose then they may be conventional clothes but I
3	probably wear them in a strange way you know in a
4	strange mixture so they always so I always you know
5	look strange to people anyway even if I was wearing
6	conventional clothes and it went on really
7	cos feeling different to everybody else
8	and what I'm wearing is a way of expressing
9	the isolation really you know
10	if if you felt isolated from everybody else
11	then once you get to the age where you can choose

12   for yourself then I would choose to wear clothes
13   where II could show that I felt differently
14   to everybody else around me
15   so that's how I started doing it

In this extract, Tony's statement, 'ever since I started wearing clothes which I chose' (lines 1–2), could constitute a perfectly adequate account of change. It seems reasonable that change to unconventional appearance comes with one's ability to choose one's clothes rather than, say, wearing those provided by one's parents. What is interesting about Tony's utterance is that he does not terminate his description at this point. Instead he goes on to say that 'they may be conventional clothes but . . . I always look strange to people anyway' (lines 2–5). He simultaneously switches from the past to the present tense, from 'ever since' and 'I started' to 'they may be'. This switch suggests two things. First, that there is something problematic about accounting for change in terms of choice of clothing, and that what follows his initial statement constitutes an attempt to avoid this problem. Second, it suggests that what he says is not only applicable to the past, or to the period of change, it is also relevant to the present. It is worth examining Tony's utterance in some detail in order to identify the nature of the problem, and how what follows constitutes a solution to that problem.

There are three observations relevant to Tony's reformulated account. First, he says that '*they may be* conventional clothes' and later, acknowledging that his present appearance is not conventional, that '*even if I was* wearing conventional clothes' he would still appear strange to other people. In other words, they would regard him as strange in conventional and in unconventional clothing. Second, Tony provides an explanation for why this might be so. He says: 'I probably wear them in a strange way . . . in a strange mixture . . . so I always look strange to people anyway.' Third, this explanation is formulated as *probable* and therefore not necessarily the case.

There seem to be several functional effects of the way that this description is formulated. First, in relation to the first observation, the implication is that inferences regarding Tony's strangeness are not derived from his attire and he thereby undermines its significance. It seems reasonable to assume, however, that normally people who wear conventional clothing do not look strange. Tony's strangeness is therefore something that warrants an explanation. Thus, his provision of an explanation displays a sensitivity to and addresses possible incredulous reactions whilst maintaining the point that the type of clothing is not in itself significant. This is the second functional effect of his description. The remaining effects are derived from the way that the explanation is qualified as probable. Comparing this with the plausible alternative, 'I wear them in a strange way', we can suggest two functional effects of the qualified statement. First, it suggests that he derives the notion of strangeness from others' reactions. (Similarly, in lines 4–5, he says that 'I always look strange to people anyway'). Constructing strangeness from others' perspective orients to the reality of his claim. Second, this construction avoids the inference that the way he wore conventional clothes was a deliberate or motivated attempt on his part to appear strange.

I said above that Tony's reformulated account of change appears designed to overcome problematic inferences made available in the initial utterance, 'ever since I started wearing clothes which I chose' (lines 1–2). It is worth, therefore, comparing the two accounts of change. First, the initial statement suggests the significance of clothing; by contrast Tony's reformulation undermines the significance of clothing. Second, to choose something implies a conscious and hence deliberate decision on his part; it implies that change in his appearance was motivated specifically by a desire to look different or strange. This inference is not made available in his reformulation. At this point we are presented with a puzzle: if Tony's strangeness is not derived from his appearance, nor a deliberate attempt to appear so, what is it that accounts for his strangeness, and for his adoption of unconventional clothing? A solution to this puzzle is provided in the following part of this extract.

Tony says: 'cos feeling different to everybody else and what I'm wearing is a way of expressing the isolation' (lines 7–9). Thus, he suggests that his strangeness is derived from a feeling of difference, and this feeling is presented as a fact about himself. That it is a 'feeling' implies something more deep-rooted than, say, a belief that one is different. Moreover, formulating this feeling of difference in contrast to 'everybody else' and later referring to it as 'the isolation', conveys the *individual* nature of this difference; it is not shared with others. The implication is that Tony's strangeness is rooted in an inherent feeling of difference; it is not attributable to his unconventional appearance, nor to an intentional choice to be different.

In addition, Tony provides an alternative means of understanding the significance of his clothing. He says that 'what I'm wearing is a way of expressing the isolation really' (lines 8–9). Thus, he implies that his clothing is of significance merely as a vehicle of expression. Furthermore, that it is 'a way' suggests that there are potentially other vehicles of expression available. Thus, there is nothing intrinsically important about these clothes. The idea that clothing is merely a vehicle for expressing deeper feelings is reaffirmed in the final part of this extract in which Tony presents us with a hypothetical scenario: 'if you felt isolated from everybody else then once you get to the age where you can choose for yourself then ...' (lines 10–12). Grammatically, this statement should be continued in hypothetical terms: 'you would choose ...' and so on. Instead, however, the scenario is concluded with reference to his own case and hence becomes no longer hypothetical. Thus, Tony himself 'would choose to wear clothes where I I could show that I felt differently to everybody else around me' (lines 12–14). One effect of this switch is an implicit contrast between the hypothetical or general case and his own. The implication is that given a feeling of difference, some would not choose to wear unconventional clothes; instead they would try to hide their intrinsic difference. Tony, however, does not try to hide his difference. It is proposed that, through this contrast, he constructs an image of himself as, to coin Potter and colleagues' (1984) term, an 'honest soul' in so far as he lets his underlying feelings, his 'true self', shine through. It is worth noting, moreover, that in contrast to his initial statement 'ever since I started wearing clothes which I chose' (lines 1–2), this later statement implies that choice is not to do with clothing *per se*, but to do with whether you allow your feelings to be manifested through clothing. Since 'that's how I started doing it' (wearing unconventional clothing) he implies that his change in appearance was genuinely motivated by a desire to express his true feelings and self; his style is therefore authentic.

Summary of analysis

In this analysis, I have outlined three resources upon which speakers drew in their autobiographical accounts of change to unconventional appearance. First, in these accounts, change occurs in the absence of influence by relevant others. Second, these others are not named and their similarity to the speakers is limited. Finally, change is motivated by a true self which is independent of appearance, but which is expressed through appearance. I have suggested that these descriptive sequences are solutions to a problem of authenticity. That is, they are designed to address potential and negative inferences that change is motivated by a desire to conform to a particular image, or merely to copy others, and is hence insincere.

CLAIMS AND QUALIFICATIONS

Before drawing any conclusions from this research, it is useful to address some important methodological issues. It may be objected that I have presented an interpretation of two selected extracts taken from a single group discussion. I have given no indication of the frequency of the phenomena I discuss, nor have I paid any attention to the representativeness of my 'sample' (neither subjects nor material). Finally, since I have paid no attention to the context in which the 'data' were collected, how can I tell that the accounts are not peculiar to the circumstances in which they were collected, or to the interviewer who collected them? An important implication of these objections is that I can make no general claims on the basis of my analysis either about autobiographical accounts, or about the factors underlying membership of subcultures.

In a sense, these kinds of objections are misplaced: my concern was with how these autobiographies were constructed, with the resources used, and the functions thereby served. It was not my aim to identify how often these resources were used nor to address underlying causal factors. Nevertheless, it is worth addressing them directly because they are precisely the kinds of reactions with which discourse analyses are likely to be greeted. In addition, general, causal statements are often more immediately persuasive than those about specific cases.[3]

My first point relates to concerns over the context-specificity of my findings. It seems unlikely that the resources I observed were generated solely by my presence; it is more useful to regard them as culturally available resources which speakers drew upon in my presence. Therefore, the research situation can be regarded as a context in which resources and practices are elicited or used, rather than created (see also Potter and Mulkay, 1985). Moreover, there seems no good reason to suppose that the resources observed are solely a product of the interview situation. Any situation can be described in a variety of ways and it seems unlikely, especially given its roots in the realm of traditional social science discourse, that it is the characterization, 'interview situation', that is of relevance to the speakers.

Second, since I present all the material I analyse, you do not have to take my interpretations on trust; you can inspect the relevant materials to see for yourselves if my observations seem valid. Furthermore, from the analysts' point of view, knowing that an audience will be able to consult the material acts as a powerful constraint upon careless or unjustified observations (Atkinson and Heritage, 1984).

My third point is that focusing the analysis on what is said ensures that it answers to the details of actual incidents and events (in so far as these accounts are themselves events). Moreover, it can be argued that the act of changing or adopting certain features of appearance cannot be extricated from the meanings or interpretations given to that change; such meanings are constructed and negotiated in the back-and-forth flow of discussion. It is therefore appropriate to study change and its meaning in the interactional context in which both are constructed. It is worth briefly contrasting this with the more orthodox social psychological approach where, in order to establish the broad empirical laws which are commonly the goal of such work, researchers must isolate processes from the very context that gives meaning to the phenomena in which they are interested. In addition, since research is usually led by theoretically derived hypotheses, rather than observation, there is always the possibility that one is investigating fictions of one's own making (Parker and Shotter, 1990).

One advantage of the discourse analysis approach is therefore that the focus is on the ways that people themselves account for the significance of their style. A second advantage is that, because it entails talking to people, it goes some way towards giving a voice to those hitherto silenced and in this sense helps 'empower' the subjects of traditional social science research (cf. Bhavanni, 1990). There is, however, a certain irony in this approach and its objectives. In an important sense the participants themselves are irrelevant because it is the language they speak that is the site of investigation. I have taken apart what was said, subjected it to detailed examination, justified doing so with reference to often dense theoretical arguments, and presented it to a select audience; I have not handed back to my participants what they said even in an interpreted form. (This is partly a problem of doing research with passers-by.)

Moreover, there is a danger that analytic 'expertise' merely replaces scientific expertise as the means of distancing researcher and researched. It is therefore questionable whether the 'democratic' underpinnings of this approach can ever be fully realized in practice (see Deborah Marks Chapter 8, this volume, for a discussion of this problem). On the other hand, that we are 'experts' can be used to legitimate the discussion and practice of discourse analysis and related issues within the academic institutions in which we are based. There are no easy solutions to such dilemmas, but it is worth recognizing them.

Having said all this, my analysis has highlighted an alternative construction of the meaning of style to that found in the social psychological and sociological accounts outlined earlier. The analysis therefore raises wider issues in so far as it exposes the one-sidedness of the social-science accounts of subcultures and style (which have also filtered into lay discourse). It thereby renders problematic the simplicity of these accounts, and the way that they neglect the issue of authenticity. This claim deserves some justification.

In the analysis, two 'readings' of style were manifested. On the one hand, style signifies group membership and conformity; and on the other it is an expression of individuality and the true self. The first reading, which both speakers reject in their own cases, resonates with the social psychological account in so far as joining a subculture is simply a matter of adopting certain criterial attributes of the category (copying others, conforming to a particular image), and redefining the self cognitively as a member. Moreover, when situationally salient, members are said to become depersonalized or to lose their individuality, becoming instead an exemplar of that collective identity (cf. Turner *et al.*, 1987).

The analysis presented here suggests that this reading of membership and style is problematic precisely because it implies conformity and the loss of individuality and this is regarded as inauthentic. Furthermore, Rob Wooffitt and I showed how, on some occasions, this type of account is actually used as a resource to undermine some members of subcultures (Widdicombe and Wooffitt, 1990). For example, later in the interview, Tony says that the hard-core punks 'really hate the goths cos like they just say oh it's just image you know it's so image orientated and that's all it is it's really shallow'. By contrast, Tony's authenticity is warranted by the second reading of style since change was motivated by a desire to be true to his intrinsically different self. It is this latter meaning of style that is absent in the social psychological account, and hence it is one-sided.

I am not suggesting, however, that style is an individual matter of one or the other meaning; for each requires the other for its significance (cf. Billig *et al.*, 1988). That is, we can read these accounts as a protest against a 'collective' reading of style only because the latter meaning is available and potentially relevant as a means by which to understand change. Furthermore, the 'social psychological' or collective identity version is *also* used as a resource by these speakers. For example, Tony says later in the discussion:

> nobody wants to be a total individual, nobody wants to be so isolated from everybody else you know so gothic is a way of being quite individual but at least you have got a few people who might know what you mean.

Therefore, it seems more useful to regard style, its meanings and its implications as essentially a dilemma which perhaps reflects a wider, recurrent ideological dilemma of individuality versus collectivity that inheres in everyday experience and thinking (Billig *et al.*, 1988). There is no easy solution, nor is one likely without a change in the nature of society and thinking. At present, therefore, it is more appropriate to consider the rhetorical processes of negotiation and argument as people deal with this and related dilemmas in everyday social existence. The analysis presented here illustrates one way in which this dilemma is negotiated in the autobiography of change.

NOTES

1 This is not an issue of which the sociologists are unaware. Hebdige, for example, concludes *Subculture – the Meaning of Style* (1979) by conceding that it is highly unlikely that the members of any subcultures would recognize themselves in his book. On the other hand, this is not regarded as a damning criticism of the approach for its utility does not reside in its resonance with subjective experience.

2 It is perhaps useful to situate this approach in relation to similar work. In common with conversation analysis (Atkinson and Heritage, 1984), the analysis focuses on the ways that utterances are designed to perform specific activities; yet it is not as concerned with 'the technology of conversation' (Sacks, 1984: 413). In common with discourse analysis (Gilbert and Mulkay, 1984; Potter and Wetherell, 1987), the analysis concerns the constructive nature of language use; but I am not concerned with identifying interpretative repertoires *per se*. Finally, in common

with both these ethnomethodologically inspired approaches to the study of discourse, I am interested in the action-orientation of language.
3 It is important to emphasize, however, that the analysis of a specific case is by no means the only way of practising discourse analysis. Instead, one might identify common patterns, or descriptive sequences within a variety of accounts (see, for example, Drew, 1987; Widdicombe and Wooffitt, 1990). Alternatively, instead of analysing just a small section from this discussion, I could have considered how the intrinsic nature of difference is also developed in the context of an interest in the supernatural; or how issues of individuality *and* collectivity are addressed and negotiated in other parts of this and other discussions. The pursuit of a more wide-ranging analysis in the space permitted would, however, necessarily entail compromising the detail of the analysis presented here.

REFERENCES

Atkinson, J. and Heritage, J. (eds) (1984) *Structures of Social Action: Studies in Conversation Analysis*, Cambridge: Cambridge University Press.

Austin, J.L. (1962) *How to do Things with Words*, Oxford: Oxford University Press.

Bhavnani, K-K (1990) 'What's power got to do with it? Empowerment and social research', in I. Parker and J. Shotter (eds) *Deconstructing Social Psychology*, London and New York: Routledge.

Billig, M., Condor, S., Edwards, D., Gane, M., Middleton, D. and Radley, A. (1988) *Ideological Dilemmas: A Social Psychology of Everyday Thinking*, London: Sage.

Brake, M. (1985) *Comparative Youth Culture: The Sociology of Youth Cultures and Youth Subcultures in America, Britain and Canada*, London: Methuen.

Cohen, S. (1980) 'Introduction to the 1980 edn of Cohen, S. (1972)', *Moral Panics and Folk Devils*, London: MacGibbon & Kee.

Condor, S. (1989) 'Biting into the future: social change and the social identity of women', in S. Skevington and D. Baker (eds) *The Social Identity of Women*, London: Sage.

Drew, P. (1987) ' Po-faced receipts of teases', *Linguistics* 25: 219–53.

Garfinkel, H. (1967) *Studies in Ethnomethodology*, Englewood Cliffs, NJ: Prentice Hall.

Gergen, K.J. and Davis, K.E. (eds) (1985) *The Social Construction of the Person*, New York: Springer-Verlag.

Gilbert, G.N. and Mulkay, M. (1984) *Opening Pandora's Box: A Sociological Analysis of Scientists' Discourse*, Cambridge: Cambridge University Press.

Hall, S. and Jefferson, T. (eds) (1976) *Resistance through Rituals*, London: Hutchinson.

Hebdige, D. (1979) *Subculture – the Meaning of Style*, London: Methuen.

Murdock, G. (1974) 'Mass communications and the construction of meaning', in N. Armistead (ed.) *Reconstructing Social Psychology*, Harmondsworth: Penguin.

Palmonari, A., Carugati, F., Ricci Bitti, P. and Sarchielli, G. (1984) 'Imperfect identities: a socio-psychological perspective for the study of the problem of adolescence', in H. Tajfel (ed.) *The Social Dimension*, vol. 1, Cambridge: Cambridge University Press.

Parker, I. and Shotter, J. (eds) (1990) 'Introduction' to *Deconstructing Social Psychology*, London and New York: Routledge.

Pomerantz, A. (1986) 'Extreme case formulations: a new way of legitimating claims', in G. Button, P. Drew and J. Heritage (eds) *Human Studies: Interaction and Language Use*, 9: 219–30.

Potter, J. and Mulkay, M. (1985) 'Scientists' interview talk: interviews as a technique for revealing participants' interpretative practices', in M. Brenner, J. Brown and D. Canter (eds) *The Research Interview: Uses and Approaches*, New York: Academic Press.

Potter, J. and Wetherell, M. (1987) *Discourse and Social Psychology: Beyond Attitudes and Behaviour*, London: Sage.

Potter, J., Stringer, P. and Wetherell, M. (1984) *Social Texts and Context: Literature and Social Psychology*, London: Routledge & Kegan Paul.

Sacks, H. Unpublished transcribed lectures, 1964–1972, University of California, Irvine.

—— (1972) 'On the analysability of stories by children', in J.J. Gumperz and D. Hymes (eds) *Directions in Sociolinguistics: the Ethnography of Communication*, New York: Holt, Rinehart & Winston.

—— (1984) 'On doing "being ordinary"', in J. Atkinson and J. Heritage (eds) *Structures of Social Action: Studies in Conversation Analysis*, Cambridge: Cambridge University Press.

Schenkein, J. (1978) 'Sketch of the analytic mentality for the study of conversational interaction', in J. Schenkein (ed.) *Studies in the Organisation of Conversational Interaction*, New York: Academic Press.

Shotter, J. and Gergen, K.J. (eds) (1989) *Texts of Identity*, London: Sage.

Turner, J.C. (1982) 'Towards a cognitive redefinition of the social group', in H. Tajfel (ed.) *Social Identity and Intergroup Relations*, Cambridge: Cambridge University Press.

Turner, J.C., Hogg, M.A., Oakes, P.J., Reicher, S.D. and Wetherell, M.S. (1987) *Rediscovering the Social Group: A Self-categorisation Theory*, Oxford and New York: Basil Blackwell.

Widdicombe, S.M. (1988) 'Adolescent peer groups and subcultures: a social psychological analysis', unpublished D. Phil Thesis, University of Oxford.

Widdicombe, S. and Wooffitt, R. (1990) '"Being" versus "doing" punk: on achieving authenticity as a member', *Journal of Language and Social Psychology*, 9: 257–77.

Wittgenstein, L. (1953) *Philosophical Investigations*, trans. G.E.M. Anscombe, New York: Macmillan.

Wooffitt, R. (1990) 'On the analysis of interaction: an introduction to conversation analysis', in P. Luff, N. Gilbert and D. Frohlich (eds) *Computers and Conversation*, London: Academic Press.

—— (1992) *Telling Tales of the Unexpected: The Social Organisation of Factual Accounts*, London: Harvester Wheatsheaf.

Wootton, A. (1989) 'Remarks on the methodology of conversation analysis', in D. Roger and P. Bull (eds) *Conversation: An Interdisciplinary Perspective*, Clevedon and Philadelphia: Multilingual Matters.

Chapter 7

Discoursing jealousy

Paul Stenner

This chapter attempts a 'thematic decomposition'[1] of text taken from taped interviews I have conducted on the topic of jealousy with a soon-to-be-married couple, Jim and May (these are pseudonyms). It is a much condensed version of a wider research project (Stenner, 1992).

A 'thematic decomposition' is a close reading which attempts to separate a given text into coherent themes or stories. This approach is informed by the idea that discourse does not simply *express* or reflect meanings, rather, meanings are *constructed* through discourse (Potter and Wetherell, 1987). These constructions are useful and have 'cultural currency' inasmuch as they are *social* and enable a *shared* understanding. They should not, therefore, be considered as the product of any given individual. We use and adapt stories with narrative themes which have already been arranged for us (Sarbin, 1986). Such 'socially sedimented' (Berger and Luckman, 1966) stories can be well thought of as trans-individual, historically localized, culturally specific formations of language-in-use.

My approach is also informed by the post-structuralist concept of 'subject position'. A 'subject position' is a 'part' allocated to a person by the use of a story.[2] As put by Harré and Davies:

> the constitutive force of each discursive practice lies in its provision of subject positions. A subject position incorporates both a conceptual repertoire and a location for persons within the structure of rights for those that use that repertoire ... Among the products of discursive practices are the very persons who engage in them.
>
> (Harré and Davies, 1990: 43)

This chapter sets out to problematize the idea, endemic in psychology (Harré, 1986), that jealousy is an 'intrapsychic essence'; a real and unitary psychological property. The *constructionist* stance I am taking views the emotion as inseparable from the social/cultural/judgemental context of its enactment. In other words, jealousy is conceived − not as *originating* from within the mind of the individual − but as being produced within the 'interactive space' (Coulter, 1989); as a complex social production mediated and generated by culturally available knowledges. My focus is on the *storied* nature of jealousy.

Elsewhere in my research I have used other techniques (such as Q-methodology) to look at how the 'experience' of jealousy is accounted (Stenner, 1992). Here, however, attention is directed on to how the 'attribution' of jealousy (and its absence) is employed in the context of a relationship. My reading of the interview material, for instance, shows Jim using a story which positions May as jealous, and May resisting this positioning. The employment of a 'thematic decomposition' enables us to see that the question of whether or not May is 'really' jealous is not the central issue. May's jealousy is the negotiated product of a series of storied contestations. If Jim's story gains precedence over May's and becomes accepted as the 'true' definition of the situation, then he will have done something more than simply and neutrally *identifying* and labelling May's internal emotional state of being. This perspective, therefore, gives rise to a different set of theoretical and methodological questions. We must resist the urge to ask whether or not a given story is 'true', and instead look to what may be said to be *achieved* by its use. What are its constructive effects? What is it doing?

In what follows I trace through a number of subject positions set up by competing stories. The 'thematics' derived from my reading of the interview with Jim will be considered before turning to the interview with May. Note that I refer to this analysis as a *reading*, and not as my *interpretation* of what Jim and May are *intending* to say. An interpretation can be more or less accurate, − being assessed against either the authorial intent of the speaker, or against some outside truth (both criteria are problematized by post-structuralism), − a reading must be judged by how useful it is.

READING OF 'JIM INTERVIEW'

'Ideologically informed anti-jealousy'

J: I've never been jea ... I've never really believed in monogamy.

There are two parts to this first story. First, jealousy is seen as being the emotion of unenlightened, unaware individuals with outmoded beliefs.

J: No, no. Never, no. I can say that about any women ... it would never have worried me if they'd gone off with other men.

Int: So how do you feel about jealousy then, do you see it as a kind of weakness?

J: Uh ... it's one of the many things I don't understand about people. Why do they go around chopping each other up with axes and stuff? Why do they go around shooting each other when it's patently not necessary to do so? How do the very rich people feel about the grinding poverty surrounding them? Why do people get sexually jealous? ... You know, I don't understand the mass of humanity at all.

Jim (J) is positioned by his story as an 'outsider' or 'non-conformist'. It provides him with a particularly positive identity as a member of an 'ideologically sound' vanguard of enlightened individuals. The second part of the story, 'other people can't handle my ideas', concerns Jim's relations with other people (mainly women) which, within this story, are hindered by the inability of others to accept the hard truth of the unacceptability of monogamy. When asked about these relations, Jim replies:

J: Uh, Well, you know, the girl asks you what you think, you tell her what you think, she disagrees violently with you, and after a while the relationship breaks up!

Other girlfriends have been *ostensibly* like Jim, but have inevitably 'fallen short' at some juncture:

J: So it's been more like that with everybody else. To varying degrees. Subsequent girlfriends have been ... ostensibly like me, they were atheists, you know. Like May ... she's the girlfriend who's most like me, that I've ever had ... I was very surprised when she announced that we were getting married.

A contradiction

We can read an illuminating contradiction into Jim's text regarding this point. This story implies that he discusses his views on monogamy and jealousy in an up-front and open (but inevitably frustrated) manner. However, the only examples Jim gives directly contradict this impression. Did Jim mention his ideas about anti-monogamy during the early stages of his relationship with May?

J:　Well, no, umm, it was never like the primary conversation, you don't meet someone and say 'oh, who are you? what's your name? what's your feelings on sexual monogamy?'

Int:　Yeah. But was anything, like, implicit in the relationship? Like that you would be faithful in any kind of way?

J:　Yeah, it always has been, with my girlfriends, it's always been their concept, sort of thing.

Note that Jim finds it necessary to account for the fact that he made no mention to his partner of what he was previously constructing as his deep-rooted ideological commitment to anti-jealousy. He does this by making a joke of the possibility of meeting someone and instantly tackling them on questions of monogamy (Potter and Wetherell (1987: 47), call this device the 'extreme case formulation'). He uses the same strategy when describing why no mention of monogamy and fidelity was made in the marriage vows which they had jointly rewritten along 'humanist' lines:

J:　Well, we went through the detail, and, decided we'd cut out anything, like, any reference to God, the state, love, honour, and obey . . . but actually that [fidelity] never came up. I didn't say things like, 'oh sorry, that's got to go', we just built up our own thing from scratch.

So, Jim's ideologically informed stance against monogamy does not stretch to discussing these ideas with his partner. This 'contradiction' Jim addresses by use of humour and parody and by denying his own personal involvement in the monogamy. The marriage also is something which is 'forced' on him:

J:　I was very surprised when she announced that we were getting married . . . Well you know, I was . . . psychologically twisted into it. Loads of pressure really, you know.

A necessary compromise

J: Yeah. That's how I see my life, you know, making a lot of compromises.

So, Jim finds that other people fail to live up to his 'anti-jealousy' ideals. The fact that he *does* live a monogamous life and does *not* openly talk about his anti-monogamy to his partners does not prevent this positive positioning. Indeed, he is also able to position himself as a considerate compromise maker. To achieve this, Jim draws upon a multitude of resources, three of which we will briefly examine.

The first involves Jim depicting himself as being pressured on all sides to conform to 'traditional' relationship stereotypes. He can either bend in the direction of the wind of this pressure, or resist and be broken:

J: I've always been very easy going, going along with other people, especially when I'm so heavily outnumbered. Well, when you're outnumbered by your mother and father, and uh, all your relatives, and a fair number of your friends as well, you know, and you think they'd hate it if you went and did something too alternative, and the same thing with one-on-one relationships.

The second theme emphasizes what Jim would lose if he didn't compromise:

J: I could be completely open with everybody. If this wasn't going to work and she was going to throw me out of the flat, and send me back to the student bedsit or whatever, then it would be silly and it would obviously be far more sensible to lie.

The third and most significant theme of 'necessary compromise' involves Jim positioning May as someone who would be hurt and upset if he were to live by his principles of non-monogamous anti-jealousy. The clearest example of this is the following:

J: Obviously you don't want to hurt . . . you don't want to say you'll do something that's going to hurt someone you care about. So you try and express what you really think and say, and you get, and then her lower lip starts to go and then I shut up.

So, Jim would *like* to be up-front and honest with May but finds that she is too emotionally weak to cope with this honesty.

A second contradiction, and May's first subject position: 'jealous'

To maintain the plausibility of this discursive complex, it is clearly necessary for Jim to position May as someone who is jealous: someone who is fragile, unstable, emotional, and who can't handle the idea of a non-monogamous relationship. However, examples or concrete instances of this jealousy are conspicuously absent. When directly asked to describe an instance of May's jealousy he replies:

J: I mean so far, actually, it's been kind of a game, because she doesn't get genuinely [laughs] angry. Because I'm always, I've been so open about it. The fact is I've never actually been unfaithful to her yet . . . she has no problem with me announcing that I'm going out with a girl, spending a lot of time with women, coming back really late at night drunk . . . she'll ask me where I've been and I'll say I've been out with A, B, C or D, or whatever, and she's said 'Oh fine' and rolls over and goes to bed.

Jim laughs when he says that 'she doesn't get genuinely angry', probably because he recognizes that he has been systematically implying the opposite. In the first extract Jim actually goes as far as to claim credit for May's lack of jealousy. He constructs his *not lying* about going out with other women as his open honesty, thus indicating caution on *his* part about this activity. Jim is suspicious that May will be suspicious. The jealousy is always only potentially present:

J: If, for example, I went ahead and had an affair and lied to her about where I'd been at certain times, and whatever, if she found out about this, she'd probably go completely ape-shit.

Apart from this potential jealousy May seems to cope in a perfectly reasonable way with Jim's ideas and, from the examples given by Jim, she seems to be prepared to talk in a direct and honest way about them:

J: So sometimes she says jokingly, 'Oh yes, well you know, I wouldn't mind if you go and have your fling, you know, just to catch up with me', but other times, she does get, you know, really upset if I ever talk about really doing it.

Int: Does she actually get angry, get upset and talk about these feelings?

J: Mmm. no not really . . . She'll keep quiet, yeah. And make it clear, let me know, you know, body language.

Jim's first subject position: 'walking on eggshells'

Jim is positioned by his story as someone who has to tread a very careful line between his own desires and the negative effect these will have on other people (particularly May). It is Jim as much as May who is hypersensitive to the ways in which his actions might influence May. He constructs a familiar position for himself where it is as if he is 'walking on eggshells'; he has the power either to hurt or to protect May by his actions. This 'power-positioning' is clearly in evidence when Jim describes feeling 'guilt if not jealousy', indicating that he sees himself as *responsible* for May's feelings:

J: Yeah, she just goes very very quiet, lower lip starts to tremble.

Int: And how does that make you feel then?

J: Well that makes me feel guilty. I do know guilt, if not jealousy.

This is a good example of the way in which emotions can be constructed through the positions made available in discourse. Jim's guilt is part and parcel of the story he is telling which allocates to him responsibility for May's supposedly fragile feelings.

Jim's second subject position: 'selfless person blown about by the winds of everyone else's desires'

The position Jim constructs for himself using 'necessary compromise' is that of a selfless individual willing to sacrifice his own desires in favour of those of other people. He constructs an identity which is in a state of permanent existential 'drift'. He drifts into monogamy by allowing it to become implicit in the relationship (see p. 117), and the marriage also is not *his* idea, in fact it goes against his principles, but still he 'drifts' into it:

J: I'm just going along with it to keep everybody else happy
. . . I'm prepared to keep my mouth shut and smile happily.

When questioned about this construction of selfless drift, Jim answers:

J: Yeah, I get the distinct impression that's been the story of
my life, as it were. I was always a good boy, do what his
mummy tells him, even when I was a kid, and I . . . went
alternative lifestyle, I didn't really go that, you know, I never
ran away from home, I always, worked hard and did well at
exams, got to university, and yeah, I've always been very
easygoing, going along with most other people, especially
when I'm so heavily outnumbered.

The joint product of these stories is a state of affairs where Jim
constructs himself as effectively paralysed. He cannot move for fear
of hurting sensitive others and so his desires become 'frozen' and
his will placed into the hands of emotionally and ideologically weak
others. An extreme synthesis of this can be seen in an extract where
Jim goes so far as to describe himself as a suffering martyr whose
selfless altruism will surely one day be repaid. How long will Jim
compromise?

J: God knows, umm. I'm optimistic, I mean, May might come
round to my way of thinking. If she gets bored of me sexually,
can't be long now! It's been three years. Uh, I'll . . . I do
keep encouraging her. And she does know I'm unhappy quite
a lot of the time. Again, maybe she'll start suffering a bit to
help me out. It's possible.

Jim's future is in May's hands:

J: The funny thing is me encouraging her to go and have affairs
so I won't feel guilty and have all my friends spit on me.

Jim's position of 'paralysis' in these stories prevents him from living
by his ideological principles and pursuing his non-monogamous
desires. It leaves him two 'passive' alternatives: (i) 'encouraging' May
to act as *he* would like to (as above); and (ii) criticizing and undermining her reasons for not acting as he would like to. He sets about
the second by use of what Wendy Hollway (1989) calls 'the permissive discourse', which argues for a sexuality 'freed' from
monogamy. This story is seen by Hollway as a reaction to the
'have/hold' construction of relationship which stresses commitment
in the form of sexual 'faithfulness'. May is positioned by Jim as a

believer in the 'have/hold' story. The 'permissive discourse' can be seen as taking one of the central tenets of the 'have/hold'; discourse; that sex and the emotions should never be separated, and subjecting it to a critical attack. 'Have/hold' subjects are constructed as being *unable* to separate sex and emotions: they have an insecure and disabling *need* to keep them together.

The permissive discourse

J: Having a stable relationship in my eyes, shouldn't have anything to do with sexual faithfulness. It's like, disappearing for three days at a time and not telling her where you're going, that kind of thing . . . that's unreasonable, that's unstable . . . May doesn't mind how many women I see as long as I don't sleep with them. It's bizarre, because I can tell them everything, exchange the deepest darkest secrets of our soul, but as long as there's no touching involved, it's absolutely fine and dandy which is strange isn't it? . . . I mean I've got these really close friends who happen to be women, and, for example, I see John from time to time . . . and the fact that I've gone away with someone, and we ended up sleeping in the same room together . . . and like we're really close friends other . . . you know she's not jealous about John at all! Presumably because there's no sex involved. It's utterly incomprehensible to me . . . I've got some other close friends more recently in London who also happen to be extremely attractive women. So would it matter if in addition to being really close friends I went to bed with them from time to time? Or not? I really can't understand that attitude.

Note that the emphasis is placed on what should *not* be the case, critiquing the 'have/hold' by emphasizing its contradictions. He describes what he thinks really *is* damaging to relationships, and he problematizes the core of the 'have/hold' discourse (which separates sex out as a unique, central and highly significant act) by stating that it is 'bizarre' and 'strange isn't it' that you can have lunch with someone and talk intimately, but not have sex or physical contact with them.

So, in this passage, Jim elaborates upon his ideologically informed anti-jealousy by using the 'permissive discourse' without having to make *his* desires explicit. Again, Jim is being 'blown about by the winds of other people's desires'. He is at the mercy of the traditional, moral and arbitrary rules of other people. Rules from which Jim is careful to distance himself: 'I really can't understand that attitude, it's utterly incomprehensible to me, you know.'

There is something peculiar about this story, however. Implicit within it is a theme which is never directly stated and which does not bring with it the subject position of moral exemplar. Is there really no difference for Jim between his close male friends and his other friends who 'happen to be extremely attractive women'? The impression generated is that *primarily* they are 'really close friends', and only secondarily 'extremely attractive'. One is *added* to the other. The following section is also interesting in this respect:

J: I've got a lot of female friends, you know, friends who happen to be female, and have lunch with them, and see them after work . . . . And like, the job I used to have, there was a big bunch of people I got on well with, some were women, and I'd go out for drinks with the old gang and sometimes there'll be one woman and lots of men, and stuff like that, and uh, she always makes jokes about the fact that I have lunch with extremely attractive women . . . One or two of which I would extremely like to sleep with. They are extremely attractive.

Notice that in the first half of this extract great care is taken to emphasize the gender-neutral 'friendly' aspects of his acquaintances: 'the old gang', 'people I got on well with, some were women'. The second half of the passage, by contrast, indicates that the gender of these people is not in fact irrelevant; indeed the word 'extremely' is used three times in the last three lines to express the extent to which Jim is physically attracted to these 'female friends, you know, friends who happen to be female'.

A closer look at the text suggests that we can identify a further story, only ever indirectly stated, which holds that the point of a relationship is primarily sex.

A 'laddish' construction of sexuality

Why does Jim involve himself in such relationships?

J: Well. First of all you're trying to lose your virginity, aren't you? Yeah! Then you make sure that you kind of keep on getting laid. And if you're a nice person it's always nice to have someone to talk to.

Here the order of priority found in the 'permissive discourse' is directly reversed; first there is sex, and second, 'if you're a nice person', friendship. Jim, talking here from a position in the 'laddish' story, is nevertheless clearly aware of an available discursive tension between the laddish privileging of sex and an alternative (often female) prioritizing of companionship and friendship. He distances himself from the latter at the same time as subtly mocking its 'niceness'.

READING OF MAY INTERVIEW

The companionship / friendship construction of relationships

This story, which we have already encountered as the 'other' to the 'laddish' theme, is summed up by May as follows:

M: I mean, I suppose, for myself, I just don't think of sex as being the most important thing in a relationship. I think, um, companionship, trust and all the rest of it is far more important than that for me.

So, from the start sex is constructed as being secondary to companionship. May talks of her 'companionship/friendship' construction of relationships as the product of her own self-development and maturation. She tells a familiar 'maturity story' which charts her development from a person unable to communicate openly (and therefore prey to jealousy) to a person able to communicate openly (and therefore no longer jealous).

From the old May to the new May

'Communication' forms the axis of this transition. May spends some time talking about an earlier, 'immature' relationship where she describes feeling intensely jealous. She refers to this affair as 'a closet relationship' and explains her jealousy as being the product of an extreme lack of communication compounded by lack of self-worth. This lack of communication May describes as a 'gap' which she filled with her own 'self-punishing' jealous thoughts. Did this jealousy stem from a lack of communication?

M: Yes (loudly), oh, I think so, yes . . . Because . . . it meant that in a way you could . . . you could and you did perpetuate both sides of the conversation in your own mind.

The 'new May' is more able to communicate and thus no longer jealous:

M: It was years . . . before I could have, sort of the happy-go-lucky attitude I have now about relationships.

M: I certainly haven't ever felt any jealousy in regard to [Jim], in fact it's been nothing but sort of obnoxious, content sort of feelings really.

So, using this 'maturity story' which culminates in the adoption of the companionship/friendship story of relationships, May is able to position herself as a mature, 'healthy', and above all *experienced* or worldly person.

May's second subject position: 'a person of experience'

M: I suppose I've been a very experiential learner, I've learnt the hard way through everything and I . . . I think I was a lot more rebellious . . . and the outcome of that was that I did experience . . . have sexual experiences much younger than Jim . . . and many more, before serious relationships and . . . a lot of things have happened to me that he knows about . . . well, I suppose it does amount to a lot packed into a few years and now in a way my only desire is to sort of like . . . I mean to me it's actually a novelty to not go out and have a wild time.

This subject position could not be in starker contrast to the one constructed for her by Jim. In his story she was positioned as an emotionally weak and jealous individual who cannot handle Jim's ideas or intentions and who (rather like a fragile eggshell) needs to be protected from knowledge that she is unable to bear. In May's story she comes across as a kind of battle-scarred and unshockable figure who has absorbed every blow that society can deal to her. She makes a point of asserting that, in principle, nobody should be 'protected' by somebody else from life's experiences:

M: I certainly feel that I've burnt my fingers enough times . . . I do believe in experiential learning and I don't think that you can prevent people from hurt and pain and . . . grief and anguish and . . . regrets. I don't think that you can protect them and you shouldn't. But those who have maybe been protected through life longer or had a generally very comfortable existence — there might be something in them that

> still makes them want to ... you know, something like
> they're never quite satisfied like. ... restless or itchy feet.
> They want to do something. They don't know the potential
> in them.

The last few sentences from this extract are an early example of the
subject position provided for Jim in this 'experience story'. He is
positioned as someone who has 'been protected through life longer
or had a generally very comfortable existence', someone with 'restless
or itchy feet' who doesn't 'know the potential in them'. His
'inexperienced' position in relation to her 'experienced' one is made
clearly manifest in what I will call the 'catching-up' story, where
May accounts for Jim's dissatisfaction with monogamy in terms of
his limited sexual (and general) history.

'Catching up' – and Jim's third subject position: 'inexperienced'

M: If he had ... a few sexual experiences with other people
because there was sort of a burning need in him to fulfil these
sort of, you know, experience wider afield, because I think,
you know, his experience has been more limited than mine,
maybe there's this feeling of catching up or something. Then,
um, I don't think, I don't think I'd see that as damning to
our relationship.

According to this story, May has been an experiential learner whilst
Jim hasn't, and this leaves Jim with a 'burning need' to 'experience
wider afield'. Notice that one of the things that this story accomplishes
is the construction of Jim's desire for sexual experience outside of
their relationship as very much a *phase* or transitory stage in his life,
rather than an enduring state of desire or a principle. Recall that
one of the effects of the 'permissive discourse' is to construct the
person who wants to keep 'sex and emotions together' as someone
with an *inability* to make this separation. In May's story, by contrast, the person who *wants* to make this separation is constructed
as someone who is inexperienced and not mature enough to
recognize the importance of communication. The urge for 'pure
sex' or 'pure experience' is simply a stage:

M: I do get a strong sense that there is a sort of a need to mature
and go through this stage and that sounds cruel, but there is

a need to go through all this, and far be it from me to get in his way.

By using the 'experience' and the 'catching-up' stories, May is able plausibly to maintain her allegiance to the companionship/ friendship construction of relationships whilst at the same time allowing Jim a certain amount of sexual 'flexibility'. May, therefore, constructs herself as very much in control of the situation. She is not *jealous* about Jim's 'urge', rather, she is, as befits the mature and experienced teller of this story, tolerant and understanding. When asked about the possibility of Jim having 'extra-relational sex' she replies:

M: Well I think, um, it's a genuine possibility . . . I think that I would find it very sad if I let that . . . come between us, because I . . . see this sort of need in everyone to live out their lives and . . . he should do that.

A point of tension

The discursive complex so far outlined is clearly at odds with that used by Jim. How is it that people can unknowingly entertain such contrasting constructions of themselves and their relationships? One answer to this is that we falsely assume that we are in agreement if we are not in disagreement. This is compounded by the fact that, despite the importance for May of open communication, Jim does not tend to talk about his feelings and desires:

M: I try to talk to him about everything, I mean I don't think we have great secrets, but, he's not a great talker . . . I find the need to talk about things that he would never need to talk about, and so it's a bit one-sided that way, . . . it's like trying to get blood from a stone.

It is within this context that May tells a further story which is sometimes at tension with the others, and which brings with it two new subject positions. The story is 'pro-monogamy' and the positions are, for May, one of 'vulnerability', and for Jim, one of 'honesty'.

An initial indication of a 'point of tension' between these stories is provided by a textual contradiction. At one point May denies that there is any 'genuine fear' behind her jokes about Jim's 'other women':

M: I joke all the time about, you know – the other women, and
I think a lot of this joking is sort of, you know, keeping the
light-heartedness in things anyway, I don't think it comes from
a genuine fear, I have to say that.

Yet earlier she states the exact opposite:

M: But I mean the fact that it's in a jokey way, I think, behind
that joke is a sort of slightly genuine fear.

Of course, by itself such a contradiction is scant evidence for the
existence of a discursive tension; people can hardly be expected to
be non-contradictory. To demonstrate here that May is in 'two
stories' rather than in 'two minds' we need to describe more fully
the stories involved.

From 'companionship/friendship' to 'pro-monogamy'

The companionship/friendship story alone does not necessarily
involve the enunciation of a theme of 'pro-monogamy'. In May's
text, however, it is extended to incorporate monogamy:

M: I think the main thing is that your commitment emotionally
should always be to one person.

The fact that these stories are separable (you can have a version of
each without anything to do with the other) produces the possibility
for the discursive tensions and contradictions which are present in
May's text. Let us turn to the new subject position made available
to May, that of 'insecure person'.

May's third subject position: 'insecure'

M: We've been affected by our inherited backgrounds, so I'm sort
of very pro-monogamy, not for the reasons of, um, morality,
but simply for reasons of security, I'm a very insecure person,
basically. I suppose I see the fact that I'm making a commitment to him and him only as being . . . that, it's like all or
nothing.

Note that May stresses that her 'pro-monogamy' stems not from
'morality' but from what she sees as emotional necessity. The position that May here provides for herself, therefore, alters from the
previous positive, mature and sensible identity, to a more negative,

immature and 'insecure' position within the 'pro-monogamy' story. When May constructs herself as insecure this extends to her feelings about herself and her 'sexuality', she worries that she is perhaps not exciting enough:

M: I suppose my only fear is, is it going to be a problem in the future? Is Jim going to sort of one day turn around and think 'Oh God, I wish I had a more exciting wife' or something, you know?

May's previous understanding and accepting attitude towards a future Jim sexual liaison is transformed into a self-blaming, negative and emotional reaction reminiscent of the 'old May' (p. 124):

M: I don't think I'd feel jealousy *against* that other person because ... I tend to see ... it more in terms of the act, I see it more in terms of ... well you know he's turned elsewhere, I'm not good enough, I'm a terrible person and all that ... so I think I'd take it against myself.

Jim's fourth subject position: 'honest person'

Jim's positioning as 'honest' is complementary to May's positioning as insecure. May's ideal of companionship and friendship rests upon a shared commitment which, ideally, is established and maintained by open communication. Jim's reluctance to communicate disables this way of ensuring commitment, and a 'promonogamy' story provides an alternative index: that of sexual faithfulness. May's monogamy story, therefore, constructs a precarious line of 'trust':

M: I'm making a commitment to him and him only ... it's like all or nothing ... I can only feel secure if I know ... that there is commitment on both sides that is equal.

Within this story 'honesty' (by necessity) replaces communication and becomes valorized as the most important aspect of a relationship. It ranks higher even than fidelity:

M: I hope that he'd come out and tell me ... I could even live with certain things so long as there was honesty there.

Against this background Jim is constructed as an 'inherently honest person':

M: I think he also does know that ... I require honesty. And I think also that he's an inherently honest person, and I know from certain things in the past that he does come out with that um, he can't beat about the bush ... if something's on his mind he will just come out and say it. I couldn't live with somebody if I thought there was going to be suspicion.

As with Jim's proof of May's jealousy, 'body language' is resorted to as the final proof of the construction:

M: I feel that there is enough body language communication between Jim and I that I would know ... I mean I'd know for a start if he was hiding anything from me. Even though he doesn't talk about these things.

DISCUSSION

A point to be re-emphasized regarding 'discoursing jealousy' is that it is a *reading* of an interview. There is great danger of *misinterpretation* if I am taken as saying something like 'this is what is *really* going on between Jim and May'. Two points are worth making regarding this issue. First, it must be acknowledged that my reading could (and should) be re-read and similarly 'thematically decomposed' to show (or make a reading of) *my* particular concerns in engaging in this work. I am grateful to both Rex Stainton-Rogers and Maria Pini for doing exactly this the moment I began getting 'delusions of reality' on first writing this chapter. Second, the reading of 'discoursing jealousy' as if it were a finished definitive statement must be resisted. Such a decomposition is always *located* – it always comes from some 'position' and is, therefore, always–already incomplete. In this work I was interested only in bringing out relevant *constructionist* points relating to jealousy (although my focus was also influenced by those themes which I recognize from my own experience of relationships).

These issues point also to the key problem of the *place* of such work in social science. To put it crudely, I feel that work of this kind *cannot be understood* from within the framework of objectivist/ essentialist social science. If the reader believes there to be a 'reality' in the situation under study, then an approach such as 'thematic decomposition' can only ever be trivial. If the constructionist stance is embraced, on the other hand, then this approach is making a useful contribution to a highly complex subject matter.

There are, finally, the *ethical* problems. In work such as this I am painfully aware of having power and control over other people's words and, what is more, to be doing this without the (misconceived) reassurance of an objectivist methodology to back me up. Like most people, I have experienced the irritation, or even horror, of having someone else take control over the 'meaning' of my words. It is crucial to stress the importance, not only of confidentiality, but of a realization on the part of the researcher of the possible ethical minefield into which they are wandering.

This thematic decomposition, whilst making no claim to be exhaustive, represents a specific example of the enormous complexity of meaning which weaves in and out wherever jealousy is discoursed. We have seen how Jim and May draw upon numerous, often contradictory and competing stories, within which they position themselves and one another. At times their stories meet and are in agreement: May's 'pro-monogamy' and 'insecure' stories, for instance, are complicitous with Jim's 'permissive discourse' in producing the subject position of 'jealous May', and, in contradiction, both Jim and May concur with the 'catching-up' story where Jim is positioned as inexperienced, and May as (conditionally) non-jealous. At other times their stories 'clash' and are antagonistic: May's 'companionship/friendship' story with Jim's 'necessary compromise', to give just one example.

These stories, which are variously resisted, insisted upon, agreed and ignored should not be thought of as being *about* the relationship, *reflective* of emotions or *expressive* of May's or Jim's 'personality', – as if a reality existed independently beneath the discourse – but rather as *constructive* of the relationship, *productive* of contradictory and non-essential identities and *generative* of emotional experience. This realization renders problematic the 'social hygienist' assumption that such non-congruous subject positions are resolvable by, for example 'getting in touch with our feelings' or 'getting it all out into the open'. Such prescriptions can themselves be seen to be constructions located in local and contingent discourse (Foucault, 1981, makes a similar point using the example of the confession). To reduce jealousy down to a timeless emotional essence is not a route to getting beneath 'mere' discourse, but yet another type of jealousy story. Attempts to ground experience in the certainty of feelings and their vicissitudes are therefore strongly challenged. However, to end with a caveat, just as we need not conceive of emotion as lying behind discourse, so, reflexively, we are not obliged to think of the stories or thematics highlighted in this decomposition as lying behind the text itself.

NOTES

1   Thanks to Rex Stainton Rogers for this concept which avoids the 'structuralist connotations' of the notion of 'discourse analysis'.
2   Here it must be noted that people using the concept of 'subject position' go to great pains to distinguish it from the more static concept of 'role' (see Harré and Davies, 1990).

REFERENCES

Berger, P.L. and Luckmann, T. (1967) *The Social Construction of Reality*, Harmondsworth: Penguin.
Coulter, J. (1989) *Mind in Action*, Cambridge: Polity Press.
Foucault, M. (1981) *The History of Sexuality*, vol. 1, Harmondsworth: Penguin.
Harré, R. (ed.) (1986) *The Social Construction of Emotions*, Oxford: Basil Blackwell.
Harré, R. and Davies, B. (1990) 'Positioning: the discursive production of selves', *Journal for the Theory of Social Behaviour* 20: 43–63.
Hollway, W. (1989) *Subjectivity and Method in Psychology: Gender, Meaning and Science*, London: Sage.
Potter, J. and Wetherell, M. (1987) *Discourse and Social Psychology: Beyond Attitudes and Behaviour*, London: Sage.
Sarbin, T. (ed.) (1986) *Narrative Psychology: the Storied Nature of Human Conduct*, New York: Praeger.
Stenner, P. (1992) *'Feeling Deconstructed?* With particular reference to jealousy'. Unpublished Ph.D. thesis, University of Reading.

Part III

Discourse, action and the research process

Chapter 8

Case-conference analysis and action research

Deborah Marks

This chapter investigates the feedback session to participants of an earlier education case conference and the attempt to share a discourse analytic understanding of that conference with its participants.[1] The first section describes the purpose of education case conferences and why the discourse analysis project was set up. The second section discusses the motivation for feeding back the analysis and the issues this raises for those interested in empirical and critical discourse research. The third section examines the fruits of this enterprise, assessing the specific advantges and disadvantages of sharing discourse analysis with the participants of the research.

BACKGROUND: CASE CONFERENCES AS 'DISTORTED COMMUNICATIONS'

In 1974 the expansion of multiprofessional assessment became the express aim of the British Department of Education and Science. Growing emphasis was placed on the need to integrate people with 'special needs' into the community (Sines, 1988). Such a policy required co-operation between the various branches of the social services. It was in this context that multiprofessional case conferences have come to take on increasing importance in Britain in recent years, for example, in social work (Robinson, 1978), clinical psychology (West and Spinks, 1988) and social service management.

In 1978 the Warnock Report linked the concept of multi-professional assessment to education. The aim of education case conferences is to provide educational professionals (and other welfare professionals) and parents with the opportunity to meet and determine the nature of educational provision for a particular child. For instance, a conference might be arranged if a head teacher of a school feels that a pupil is in need of some form of special education.

The 1981 Education Act gave local education authorities a new strategic role in arranging a complex range of services in meeting individual special education needs (Goacher *et al.*, 1988: 46). The consultative process was developed further by the Fish Committee (1985), which advocated that the school, relevant professionals, pupils, parents and the child work towards integration into all aspects of school and community life.

Despite being presented as a panacea for ensuring a balanced debate in the social-service decision-making machinery, reports from educational psychologists (MacIntyre and Burman, 1987), parents (Heard, 1987; Reepers, 1989) and reports from the Department of Education and Science indicate that case conferences are fraught with communication difficulties and conflict. It has been argued that such meetings serve merely to rubber-stamp professional interests (Ford *et al.*, 1982) rather than to engage in open debate. Moreover, since the Education Reform Act (1988), new strains have been placed on interprofessional co-operation. The Act increases pressure on school managers to improve academic results (and weakens the jurisdiction of local education authorities) providing inducement to schools to have 'difficult' children placed in special schools. This conflicts with the educational psychologist's aim to integrate children with special needs.

The impetus for a discourse analysis of education case conferences came from the observation that children from manual working-class and West Indian parentage were over-represented in special schools (Tomlinson, 1982). Case conferences may confirm some practices of schools and allied educational services in reproducing patterns of disadvantage along class, ethnic and gender lines (Eggleston *et al.*, 1987). For example, by focusing on the child as a 'problem', rather than critically examining classroom interactions or socioeconomic factors, the case conference may reinforce a number of other signifying practices, such as the way in which educational pedagogies and classroom practices reproduce socioeconomic relations (Sharp and Green, 1975; Willis, 1977). Case-conference discourses help to structure the way in which a child's educational 'needs' come to be determined.

The case conference

The education conference which was examined was that of a

14-year-old black boy at a comprehensive school. The boy, who will be referred to as Mike, displayed (according to comments made by professionals) behavioural problems caused by 'difficulties at home'. Mike's teachers felt that he could no longer be managed within the school. For this reason a meeting of his parents, teachers and other (white) welfare professionals was called to discuss the possibility of his removal from his current comprehensive school into special education.

At this case conference professionals debated specific ways of catering for his needs. However, a discourse analysis of this meeting (Warren, 1988) challenged the way professionals defined the issues and failed to leave a space for Mike and his parents to contribute to the debate. In place of the idealized model of interprofessional communication at education case conferences, it was suggested that different interest groups in the case conference employed a variety of rhetorical devices to achieve specific interests.

APPROACH AND RATIONALE

Two years on: the feedback meeting

Two years after this study was carried out two psychology lecturers and a research assistant (myself) met with educational professionals (the teacher and education welfare officer) from Mike's original case conference together with Mike and his mother. The participants were brought together by the educational psychologist who had set up the case conference. The meeting took place in a classroom at the school Mike had attended. At the start of the meeting the educational psychologist and two of the researchers took about one hour to describe the aims of the research into education case conferences and the reasons for setting up the feedback meeting.

The purpose of this meeting was to share our analysis of the way in which language was organized into sets of statements or discourses with participants of the earlier research. This would achieve the following objectives.

First, it would deepen our understanding of the way in which case-conference discourses were rhetorically organized within a specific context. By bringing people together to examine the way they conceptualized the issues at the original case conference it would be possible to show that the divergent 'attitudes' of participants are not fixed entities in the way that many social psychologists would have us believe. Having had two years' distance from the involved exchanges of the original case conference, it was hoped that participants would be able to generate new ways of talking about the meeting which would undermine the image of them as autonomous 'subjects' with beliefs held independent of context.

The feedback meeting would provide the opportunity to carry out a piece of 'action research' which would eschew the positivist objective of 'observation' without intervention. The meeting would explicitly acknowledge the way in which theoretical categories do not refer to neutral external 'real' objects, but actually help to constitute these objects. For example, criteria for defining educational ability has changed through history and is applied differentially among social groups. The socially constructed nature of educational assessment generally, and special education in particular, has been well-documented (Croll *et al.*, 1984; Rose, 1985; Bowman, 1986; Elliot, 1987; Billig *et al.*, 1988).

Second, sharing our interpretation of case–conference discourses with participants of the feedback meeting would impact directly on their lives. By recognizing this and attempting to collaborate with teaching professionals in critical reflection we aimed to avoid exploiting our professional participants by 'extracting' our 'material/data' from them and then withdrawing to 'write it up'. We had stated at the outset our desire that participants should find the research useful for their professional practices. The teachers and the psychologist had stated their interest in our 'findings' and their openness to new ways of seeing. In this way the benefits of the project would thus not simply accrue to ourselves as researchers interested in discourse analysis and educational policy. A commitment to share the fruits of research with participants of the original case conference had been made in 1988. Such a collaborative approach has become an important strand within qualititative and educational research (see Carr and Kemmis, 1986).

In addition to the critical impulse *vis-à-vis* challenging professional practices, we were also concerned with the liberatory goal of empowering the subject of the case conference. Critical reflection on language would expose the dominant ways of seeing in the meeting which we felt had served to regulate him. Specifically, we felt that in the case conference, Mike had had fewer rights to speak since the educational professionals took responsibility for finding a solution to his 'problems'. By exposing the way in which he was positioned in and through language, it was hoped that the feedback meeting would open a space for challenging discursive practices and for enabling Mike to resist being positioned as the 'problem'. (In a prior interview Mike had constructed 'his problem' in terms of racism in the school rather than in terms of his behaviour and home environment.)

Finally, we hoped that the process of feeding back would offer the opportunity for a reflexive analysis of the research process and our own role in case-conference discourses. This would 'democratize' the research by giving participants the opportunity to comment on our interpretations. We would explicitly recognize that there are multiple ways of conceptualizing the case conference.

Appreciation of the reflexive nature of language is a central feature of discourse analysis. By recognizing that the structure of language is not transparent 'all our claims are reflexive in a manner which cannot be avoided. For to recognise the importance of language is to do so within language' (Lawson, 1985: 9, see also Ashmore, 1989). Implicit within the discourse analytic project is the belief that, 'there is no longer any representation, there is only action, theory's action, the action of practice in the relationship of networks' (Deleuze, quoted in Kritzman, 1988: 14). This is a point which is particularly salient when discourses are identified by participant observers. However, even where the researcher is not present, she still plays a crucial role in defining a discourse. The way in which language is heard, transcribed (Ochs and Schieffellen, 1979) and organized into discourse categories involves a creative process of construction for which the analyst ought to acknowledge responsibility. Yet some discourse analysts seem to put such issues to one side, discussing their texts as if they existed 'out there', in media sources or as if they could be collected unproblematically (cf. West's (1990) discussion of hidden video cameras to collect doctor–patient discourses).

The power to identify, define and label a set of meanings which form a 'discourse' enables us to exert our power as academics to exhibit, control, classify and thus reify meaning. Yet 'our philosophical commitment to the idea that meanings emerge within a context and can be interpreted only narratively rather than objectively, envie us to become self-reflexive. Feeding back would enable us to look closely at our practice in terms of how we contribute to dominance despite our liberatory intentions' (Lather, 1986: 156). The feedback meeting would, we thought, encourage participants to challenge our interpretations and expose our own position to critical appraisal. This would allow conscious and deliberate subversion of the positivist fantasy of being a 'fly on the wall' and having no impact on the world being studied. The challenge was, as Lather succinctly puts it, to 'foreground our own perspectivity ... without putting ourselves back at the center' of the narrative, and develop 'forms of inquiry that are "interruptors" of the social relations of dominance' (Lather, 1986: 157).

Having reviewed our reasons for calling people back for a critical discussion of the original case-conference proceedings, the meeting was opened up for participants to make their contributions.

However, the aims, as delineated (in simplified form) for participants, and described earlier, seemed to be mutually incompatible. The attempt to encourage reflection and to instigate change in practices represented the clash between (postmodern) concerns to construct systems of meanings as contingent, positioned and partial with (modern) liberatory concerns to challenge social inequalities. Moreover, the goal of empowering the case-conference subject was in itself problematic since it represented collusion in the very oppressive practices we were seeking to challenge. This is because our discourses of reflection and emancipation were underscored by our privileged position as expert, professional (white, middle-class) 'discourse analysts'.

I shall illustrate some of these difficulties by discussing three discourses which I have identified. These are the 'therapeutic' discourse, the 'reflective' discourse and the 'rejectionist' discourse.

FEEDBACK DISCOURSES

The therapeutic discourse: Mike's 'needs' and our frustrations

The feedback meeting provided educationists with the opportunity to discuss their role and the problems associated with it. One central issue to emerge was the failure of the meeting to address the 'needs' of various participants. These needs were defined by the education welfare officer, Sally, who began by talking about the failure to resolve 'the situation'.

Extract 1

Sally: And we had this meeting (.) and I found that meeting very frustrating (.) ... *the situation hadn't been able to be resolved* (.) er (.) the pure fact that the person who actually isn't here today [coughs from a couple of people] who at the time was responsible in the social services department (.) er (.) wasn't able to to to *bring the situation together for Mike* to come to school and feel good about himself (.) and (.) as I do remember it quite well, my own frustrations (.)*

In this extract Sally refers to a mysterious 'situation' which could not be resolved in a general sense. This turned out to be the problem of Mike's low self-esteem and the failure of another professional from the social services to deal with it. By referring to Mike's presumed emotional difficulties in passive terms as 'the situation' no acknowledgement is given to the possible existence of competing accounts. The repetitious reference to 'the situation' serves to mask rhetorical positions by objectifying the assertion that the problem is Mike's lack of self-esteem and the solution lies in the help of the caring professions.

Mike's life is thus presented as being fragmented. Appeal is implicitly being made to the humanistic therapeutic discourse which sees the subject as being unified and integrated (see Diamond, 1991). Mike's potential helpers are empathetic towards him, and consequently, they need support and feel frustration. In this way conflict of interest between Mike and his mother and the professionals is mystified.

This focus on both Mike's and his mother's feelings (and the stresses and strains this places on the professionals) continues in the education welfare officer's account of the reason for suppressing professional differences.

Extract 2
Sally: People don't often say in meetings (.) the things they want to say because *there's this perpetual barrier to stop you* (.) because you don't want to (.) involve *other people, involve parents* (.)

* *Key to participants*		*Key to transcription*
Trevor	— teacher	(.) pause
Jane	— educational psychologist	underline emphasis
Emelia	— researcher	= overlap
Tom	— researcher	) talking at same time
Sally	— education welfare officer	
Mrs Jones	— mother of case-conference subject (Mike)	
Mike	— subject of case conference	
Kate	— researcher at original case conference	

professionals (.) professional differences *(.) that's the word* (.) I think *you're* always very sensitive to people's feelings because they're not here to listen to your differences (.) but after the case conference (.) is called (.) that's where you could actually use it, isn't it?=

Emelia: =Yes.

Extract 3
Sally: I don't think for one minute (.) any of us would get involved in professional differences (.) erm (.)

In these extracts we see the way the education welfare officer responds to the interests of the researcher by referring to communication difficulties and 'professional differences' in the case conference. However, the emphasis still remains placed on professional commitment to support Mike. The significance of professional differences is played down by her description of such disagreements as 'the word'. In this way reference to actual conflict is clouded. Moreover, she distances herself from involvement in this interprofessional conflict by talking about her own feelings in terms of 'you'; 'you don't want to' and 'you're always very sensitive'. Yet it is clear from the context that 'you' is used in the sense of 'one'; Sally is referring to herself. She thus presents herself as a 'therapist' who suppresses acknowledgement of conflict in the interests of her client. Case conferences cannot simply be democratic forums since they must also be sensitive to clients' wishes. Just as a psychotherapist focuses on the needs of the client and therefore does not verbalize his/her own conflicts, so the education welfare officer doesn't indicate to his/her clients the underlying political conflicts which guide specific outcomes out of 'sensitivity' to the client.

When attention *is* focused on interprofessional conflict, it is immediately directed back to the 'real' issue of Mike's 'needs':

Extract 4
Sally: each and every one of us I'm sure would (.) do their utmost to support Mike (.) in terms of support . . .

Mike himself is called upon by the teacher to reinforce the point that his needs were not addressed:

Extract 5
Trevor: I know they did have a pretty stormy relationship at one time didn't you Mike?=

Mike: Yes=
Trevor.   Erm (.) but it improved . . .

Extract 6
Trevor.   I think Mike was under no illusions about what (.)
          er (.) support or otherwise he was or was not receiving
          from (.) the social services (.) em (.) [to Mike] I think
          we've talked on quite a few occasions about (.) the lack
          of help you were getting (.) from (.) the social ser-
          vices . . .

By including Mike in the discussion of the 'support or otherwise' the teacher evokes Mike's collusion in the discussion and
gives him a voice. Even if Mike fails to respond verbally, reference has successfully been made to the fact that he does have
a voice. He's talked with the teacher 'on quite a few occasions'.

    When asked if parents and pupils were given enough informa-
tion, Mike criticized the amount of information he had been given
prior to the case conference. This comment however, is immediately
reformulated into an issue of trust (and sensitivity) rather than
professional (non-) disclosure.

Extract 7
Mike: (.) er it could be a bit more (.)
Jane: What kind=?
Mike: =Well you know like more description (.) you could
          describe it a bit more (.)
Sally: Right (.) What did you say about the trust thing before
          (.) people actually knowing and trusting people?
Mike: Well ye e es (.)
Sally: I think that in Mike's case . . .

The education welfare officer felt that the case conference failed
to provide sufficient support for professional participants as well
as for Mike and his mother. Unlike other case conferences (such
as social-work case conferences relating to child abuse) in which
professionals are provided with supervisory support and the opportunity to debrief, education case conferences provide no such support.
Generally, it seemed to be felt that the research interviews following the case conference, and the feedback meeting helped by
providing the space for therapeutic reflection.

Extract 8

Sally: It was only when I actually sat down with Kate and really thought about it (.) I didn't actually recognize how (.) how frustrated I was (.) coming from one meeting (.) although they were weeks apart (.) still feeling *the same situation hadn't been resolved* (.) er (.) . . .

Just as Mike needed support in order to become integrated as a 'person', so his carers needed a feedback meeting in order to offload. Mike's difficulties were thus presented in parallel with their own. He needed a voice just as they did. The feedback meeting thus had many of the trappings of a humanistic therapy group, yet its function was not merely to give participants therapeutic space. The participants of the meeting were not strangers but colleagues. Their 'reflections' would have real social implications. The professionals used the feedback meeting to place responsibility for decisions made in the case conference with the external situation which both professionals and Mike and his mother were equal subjects to. In this way power differentials between the case-conference subject and Mike were erased. For this reason the attempt to generate critical reflection in the feedback meeting was constrained by similar factors as had operated in the original case conference. Professionals needed to sustain a sense of personal efficacy and to present themselves as frustrated carers rather than figures of authority. Our attempts to 'challenge ways of seeing' and problematize the way in which needs were defined were thus not heard by educationalists.

Extract 9

Emelia: People would find it easier to say to one person who (.) I mean in Kate's position as someone who was not involved (.) er, who was not an interested party in any position (.)

In extract 9, the researcher is seduced into adopting a therapeutic discourse, describing the previous researcher as an impartial outsider who would allow therapeutic space for reflection.

Issues of reflectivity

Following her explanation of the research and the reasons for the feedback meeting the educational psychologist distributed minutes of the original case conference in order to refresh memories and facilitate discussion:

Extract 10

Jane:	I wonder *how far* these minutes (.) reflect what you remember?
Sally:	Oh, *I can remember* it very clearly (.) Yes.
Tom:	Is this *the way* you would have described it?
Sally:	It's a *fair assessment* I think (.) I remember it very well because (.) Perhaps I shouldn't be talking now (.)=
Emelia:	=No go=
Sally:	=I remember coming to this meeting . . .

Extract 10 exhibits subtle tensions between the reflective and therapeutic discourses. In generating a discussion about the difference between records and memory, Jane and Tom make the implicit assumption that there are different versions of reality, reflecting discourse analysts' concern with the symbolic representation of meaning. This is followed by reminiscences of the education welfare officer about her feelings in the case conference. Tom steps in, in order to steer the discussion back to the topic of interpretation. This serves to situate the education welfare officer's account within a variety of possible accounts. The education welfare officer, anxious to co-operate begins to adopt a more reflective style:

Extract 11

Tom:	I guess these minutes would look very different if Kate had written them.
Sally:	Would Kate be writing (.) knowing what our views [are] . . . would that perhaps affect the way she would write it? I think it would . . .
Tom:	I'm sure it would=
Emelia:	=yes (.) yes (.)

The education welfare officer indicates her appreciation of the social construction of accounts, and is rewarded with enthusiastic affirmations.

Extract 12

Sally:	actually analysing (.) what you really wanted to say but can't=
Tom:	=what (.) you didn't want to have arguments?=

Sally: =yes=
Tom: =when Mike was there?=
Sally: =right yes . . .

The therapeutic discourse of needs was thus temporarily disrupted by our introduction of a discourse on discursive constraints. This tension between therapeutic and reflective discourses occasionally emerges as manifest conflict over precisely what was said at the case conference. One example of this is when Tom summarizes some of the issues within the case conference. He refers to people thinking Mike's pride at living in an area perceived as being predominantly black was problematic:

Extract 13
Tom: another way of talking about it was um (.) about Mike being proud of being from [black area] and this became (.) and issues that was talked about at the case conference (.) I don't know whether you remember that=
Sally: =no I don't I don't=
Tom: um and it wasn't only one person that was doing that (.) but it was another way of talking about the problem . . .

Here, Tom explicitly overrides Sally's objection to the suggestion of racism. He is able to do this because of his greater rights to speak as someone who has been introduced as a researcher and who is summarizing, from a written report his 'findings'. When Sally does get a chance to come back she says:

Extract 14
Sally: I can remember the case conference that Mike was at (.) he was so distressed at that meeting (.) he was never able to lift his head up.

In this way she reasserts (in a graphic and imperative manner) the therapeutic discourse.

By implicating ourselves (as researchers with particular goals within conversation) in our discourse analysis, questions about our role in articulating and organizing discursive practices can be addressed. This focus calls into question the social relations of the research act and the problematic way in which we, as researchers, were privileging our own reflexive/empowerment perspective and presenting ourselves as experts. Our rights to speak were predicated upon our authority as 'researchers' coming in from outside.

Rejectionism as discourse?

Mike, the subject of the case conference, avoided involvement in either the therapeutic or reflective discourses. He spurned participation in the debate and seemed to sit on the margins of the meeting. There is an interesting juxtaposition of a set of affirmatives expressed by the educational professionals, followed by Mike's negative response to the question of whether he appreciated the existence of interprofessional tensions. This serves to underline his role as outsider in his own case conference and challenges the ideology of equal exchange of information among all parties. Mike's silence through most of the discussion testifies to his refusal to participate.

Extract 15

Sally:	Would you be able to say I'm not happy about about that? (.) as a young person? [addressed to Mike] (.) Sorry (.) Do you think it would not be very easy? [addressed to Mrs Jones]
Mrs Jones:	No.
Jane:	Would you agree with that Mike or do you think (.) taking yourself back to who you were and not who you are now (.) but as a pupil (.) to actually say 'I'm not happy (.) I'm concerned with the way Jane and Sally or the school are treating me (.) I disagree with what you say.'
Mike:	Well mostly I could show that anyway.
Jane:	That's how you felt?
Mike:	Well most times yes.
Jane:	Did you feel able to say that?
Mike:	I could say it but I just didn't want to=

Mike's failure to confirm that he had difficulties in expressing himself is a source of disquiet for the adult participants. Being concerned to give the subject of the feedback meeting (the person with least status and power) a voice, it is disconcerting to have this offer to speak turned down. Mike's assertion that he positively chose not to speak is then disregarded by the researchers and educational professionals.

Extract 16

Jane:	=Is that=
Trevor:	I was going to say that I think it was probably on a one (.) or in a small situation when Mike would say=

Jane: Yes=
Trevor: He's not happy with this and going back to Sally's
            point (.) I think *Mike* was under no illusions about what
            (.) er support or otherwise he was or was not receiving
            from (.) the social services (.) em (.) [to Mike] I think
            we've talked on quite a few occasions about (.) the lack
            of help *you* were getting (.) from (.) the social services
            (.) um (.) but as Sally said that's not something that's
            brought up in a meeting (.) in a case conference and is
            not thrashed out . . .

Trevor moves from a description of Mike's understanding of
the situation, to a reference to his discussions with Mike which
incorporate Mike, to directly addressing Mike. The therapeutic
discourse of need is thus asserted with Mike's silent endorsement.
This effectively challenges the agenda of empowerment and reflection and renders invalid Mike's claim that he positively chose not
to speak rather than was unable to speak. The possibility that he
rejected the fundamental tenets of the debate (that he had 'special
needs' which had not been addressed by the social worker) was
overridden.

The above inference about the meaning of Mike's 'strategy'
of silence is, however, problematic on two counts. First, by
describing his non-participation or refusal as a strategy of opposing the therapeutic and reflective discourses we are sabotaging
his aim to distance himself from a white middle-class regulatory enterprise which does not involve him. Bhavnani (1990)
has spoken of the importance of silence as a form of resistance,
and Mike's role in the case conference serves to underline his
resistance to 'empowerment' by others. By interpreting Mike's
silence as opposition to therapeutic and reflective discourses
we were effectively undermining and sabotaging his resistance
to professional gaze. Our attempts to empower Mike in the
feedback meeting can therefore be seen as patronizing and oppressive.

Second, there are theoretical problems with conceptualizing
Mike's refusal to speak as a 'discourse'. While it is important to
recognize that silences are meaningful, it becomes problematic to
suggest that silence 'constructs an object' (Foucault, 1972; Parker,
1990). Whilst language analytically fixes and constructs subjects as
autonomous selves, silence in this instance can be interpreted as an

attempt to resist unitary wholeness. In this way, it is problematic to characterize silence as a discourse.

Problems with feeding back: reflections, realities and irony

Potter (1988) has spoken of the futility of analysing the readings of those people whose discourse we are analysing. He argues that this merely produces a proliferation of versions. He argues that it does not resolve the issue of reflexivity since there is no principled difference between our readings of the original extract and our readings of participants' readings of the extract. The attempt to draw attention to our own role in the construction of our data implies that the more reflexive we are, the more progressive our work is. Such an approach leads to navel gazing and a competitive struggle 'to be more reflexive than thou'.

The attempt to foster an ideal speech situation in which professionals and educational consumers could engage in undistorted communication (Habermas, 1970) was thwarted by the continued expression of mutually incompatible discourses (see Ellsworth (1989) for a critique of Habermasian attempts to establish genuine dialogue of differences out of conflicting subject positions). The feedback meeting seemed closer to a repetition of the positions adopted during the case conference.

This problem is hardly surprising given the context of the feedback meeting and the way in which people's interpretation of its purpose was structured by their different roles in the meeting. The feedback meeting took place in the same setting as the original case conference. When the teacher (Trevor) arrived at the classroom he asked, 'Is this Mike Jones's case conference?'. The feedback meeting was seen as a rerun of the original case conference. Interprofessional rivalries, resource shortages, the need to defend against hostility from the government, media and a variety of parent groups required educational professionals to adopt a defensive posture. Thus, attention was directed towards the child as 'the problem'.

An emphasis on Mike's 'needs' seemed actually to be built into the structure of both the case conference and the feedback meeting. Such meetings focus on specific individuals rather than the approach of the school or other socioeconomic factors. In order to achieve effective critical reflection and to generate new ways of seeing, it is not enough just to attempt to spontaneously encourage people to reflect on ways of speaking. Discursive practices emerge within specific power/knowledge contexts.

Real collaboration requires the creation of a space within which people can step outside their everyday positions, which are materially constrained. Otherwise our attempt to foster a liberatory discourse remains within the realm of idealism. Pseudocollaboration reinforces the problematic power differential between academics who gain (publications, research grants) from the project and educationalist and education consumers who are exploited (in terms of their time and energy) by the research (see Ladwig, 1991).

This raises the problem of whether discourses are reified in our account. Have 'discourses' come to look like ideological apparatuses? The implication here is that people are imprisoned within their texts and that there is no such thing as communication, but only the battle between different, untranslatable ways of seeing.

Another problem with the feedback enterprise in discourse analysis can be heard as ironicizing (Potter, 1988). The implicitly critical way that discourse analysis scrutinizes its subjects, indicated by the fact that we do not tend to analyse the discourses of those we fully agree with, means that we tend not to take what people say seriously. Discourse analysis suspends belief in a naive realist approach to people's accounts. This means that it becomes difficult to share our discourse analysis with speakers. When we do so participants are forced into a defensive posture which makes it difficult for them to develop a critical view of the 'texts' they produce. Such a dynamic reinforces our own role as experts who can stand outside accounts. Any later attempt to graft on to this an analysis of our own subject position can operate more as tokenism to the idea of reflexivity rather than 'real' acknowledgement of our power. Grounded research and acknowledgement of engagement with the patterns of life which one is analysing is important. However, academic reflection on the construction of accounts can be tedious and narcissistic. Exploring our own reasons for carrying out a piece of research serves to place ourselves at the centre of the account and leaves us locked in an endless cycle of reflexivity.

SUMMARY AND EVALUATION

Participants at the feedback meeting interpreted the research goals in different ways. The educational professionals saw the main value of the feedback meeting as giving them the opportunity to air their grievances regarding resource limitations in the provision of special education. This is an outcome reflected in other types of action research projects in schools (see Stenhouse, 1973). The academic agenda of reflection on education discourses and research practices arose from our own job remit. Mike's agenda was to resist professional labelling which had, in the past, been the source of both punishment and support.

The difficulties of combining intervention and research have been well-documented (Morris and Rein, 1967; Cohen and Manion, 1984). The specific problems of using discourse analysis for progressive, critical and socially engaged research have received less attention (see Burman, 1991). This is because critical discourse analyses have tended to be historical (for example, Rose, 1985) or deal with texts which do not include the researcher, rather than being ethnographic. A number of problems are raised when we attempt to include ourselves in our discourse analysis. Specifically, questions around the power of the researcher as expert, the problems of empowerment of the 'oppressed' and issues of achieving reflexivity and change emerge. The value of our feedback meeting should be seen as an example of how not to do empirical liberatory discourse analysis. The problem of what to do with the feedback meeting transcripts points to an inherent problem with the whole enterprise. This is that research which is both liberatory and reflexive in its challenge to regulatory practices must be fully collaborative. If educational professionals, Mike and his mother had played an integral part in construction of the research project, on instigating self-reflection and on writing a discourse analytic critique, then we, as academics would not have been positioned as experts but rather as facilitators. Feeding back requires an egalitarian context. If this were possible we would not need to feed back.

For discourse analysis to have any critical value in drawing attention to the way in which meanings and subsequent outcomes are constructed in and through language, the analysis must be taken out of its context and examined in a non-threatening setting. Discourse analysis could be adopted as a training tool for participants of case conferences and as a strategy for criticizing case–conference management, rather than used directly to challenge participants about discourses in their own case conference. In this way the deconstruction of professional educational practices is carried out from outside. The task of developing a new culture within the system of special education lies with political action informed by critical discourse analysis rather than idealist action research projects. The question arises, then, of the relationship between discourse analysis and its uses. Is discourse analysis merely a research method or rhetorical device for justifying political struggles?

NOTE

1   This chapter is based on a research project on discourse and education case conferences with Erica Burman, Leah Burman, Caroline Barrett-Pugh, Deborah Marks and Ian Parker, funded by Manchester Polytechnic and with the support of Manchester Education Authority.

REFERENCES

Ashmore, M. (1989) *The Reflexive Thesis: Wrighting the Sociology of Scientific Knowledge*, London: University of Chicago Press.

Bhavnani, K-K. (1990) 'What's power got to do with it? Empowerment and social research', in I. Parker and J. Shotter (eds) *Deconstructing Social Psychology*, London: Routledge.

Billig, M., Condor, S., Edwards, D., Gane, M., Middleton, D. and Radley, A. (1988) *Ideological Dilemmas: A Social Psychology of Everyday Thinking*, London: Sage.

Bowman, N. (1986) 'Maladjustment: a history of the category', in W. Swann (ed.) *The Practice of Special Education*, London: Routledge & Kegan Paul.

Burman, E. (1991) 'What discourse is not', *Philosophical Psychology* 4 (3): 325–42.

Carr, W. and Kemmis, S. (1986) *Becoming Critical: Education, Knowledge and Action Research*, London: Falmer Press.

Cohen, L. and Manion, L. (1984) 'Action research', in J. Bell, T. Bush, R. Fox and S. Goulding (eds) *Conducting Small-scale Investigation in Educational Management*, London: Harper.

Croll, P., Moses, D. and Wright, J. (1984) 'Children with learning difficulties and assessment in the junior classroom', in P. Broadfoot (ed.) *Selection, Certification and Control: Social Issues and Educational Assessment*, London: Falmer Press.

Diamond, N. (1991) 'The fear of the flesh: constructions of the body', paper for Second Discourse Analysis Workshop/Conference, Manchester Polytechnic, July.

Eggleston, J., Dunn, D., Anjali, M. and Wright, C. (1987) *Education for Some: The Educational and Vocational Experiences of Some 15–18 Year Old Members of Minority Ethnic Groups*, Stoke-on-Trent: Trentham.

Elliot, R. (1987) *Litigating Intelligence: IQ Tests, Special Education and Social Science in the Court-room*, Massachusetts: Auburn House.

Ellsworth, E. (1989) 'Why doesn't this feel empowering? Working through the repressive myths of critical pedagogy', *Harvard Educational Review* 59 (3): 297–324.

Fish Committee (Report of the Committee Reviewing Provision to

Meet Special Education Needs) (1985) *Educational Opportunities for All?* London: ILEA.

Ford, J., Mongon, D. and Whelan, M. (1982) *Special Education and Social Control: Invisible Disasters*, London: Routledge & Kegan Paul.

Foucault, M. (1972) *The Archaeology of Knowledge*, London: Tavistock.

Goacher, B., Evans, J., Welton, J. and Wedell, K. (1988) *Policy and Provision for Special Education: Implementing the 1981 Education Act*, London: Cassell.

Habermas, J. (1970) 'On systematically distorted communication', *Inquiry* 13: 205–18.

Heard, D. (1987) 'Does statementing meet parental needs in north west Derbyshire?' unpublished B.Ed thesis, Manchester Polytechnic.

Kritzman, L.D. (ed.) (1988) *Michael Foucault, Politics, Philosophy, Culture: Interviews and Other Writings, 1977–1984*, New York: Routledge.

Ladwig, J.G. (1991) 'Is collaborative research exploitative?' *Educational Theory* 41 (2): Spring.

Lather, P. (1986) 'Issues of validity in openly ideological research: between a rock and a soft place', *Interchange* 17 (4): 63–84.

Lawson, H. (1985) *Reflexivity: The Post-modern Predicament*, London: Hutchinson.

Mcintyre, K. and Burman, L. (1986) 'The educational needs of black pupils', Manchester Education Committee discussion document.

Morris, P. and Rein, M. (1967) *Dilemmas of Social Reform: Poverty and Community Action in the U.S.*, London: Routledge & Kegan Paul.

Ochs, E. and Schieffellen, B. (1979) *Developmental Pragmatics*, London: Academic Press.

Parker, I. (1990) 'Discourse: definitions and contradictions', *Philosophical Psychology* 3 (2): 189–204.

Potter, J. (1988) 'What is reflexive about discourse analysis? The case of reading readings', in *Knowledge and Reflexivity: New Frontiers in the Sociology of Knowledge*, London: Sage.

Reepers (1989) *Parent Partnership: The Reepers View*, Moss Side, Manchester: The Parents Centre and Education Shop.

Robinson, D. (1978) *Schools and Social Work*, London: Routledge & Kegan Paul.

Rose, N. (1985) *The Psychological Complex*, London: Routledge & Kegan Paul.

Sharp, R. and Green, A. (1975) *Education and Social Control: A Study of Progressive Primary Education*, London: Routledge & Kegan Paul.

Sines, D. (1988) *Towards Integration: A Comprehensive Service for People with Mental Handicap*, London: Lippincott.

Stenhouse, L. (1973) 'The humanities curriculum project', in H.J. Butcher and H.B. Pont (eds) *Educational Research in Britain*, London: University of London Press.

Tomlinson, S. (1982) *Educational Subnormality: A Study of Decision-making*, London: Routledge & Kegan Paul.

—— (1982) *A Sociology of Special Education*, London: Routledge & Kegan Paul.

Warnock Report (1978) *Special Educational Needs*, Cmnd 7212, London: HMSO.

Warren, K. (1988) 'The child as problem and the child with needs: a discourse analysis of a case conference', unpublished undergraduate project, Manchester Polytechnic.

West, C. (1990) 'Not just "doctors' orders": directive-response sequence in patients' visits to women and men physicians', *Discourse and Society* 1 (1): 85–112.

West, J. and Spinks, P. (1988) *Clinical Psychology in Action: A Collection of Case Studies*, London: Wright.

Willis, P. (1977) *Learning to Labour: How Working Class Kids Get Working Class Jobs*, Hants, Farnborough: Saxon House.

Chapter 9

Against discursive imperialism, empiricism and constructionism: thirty-two problems with discourse analysis

Ian Parker and Erica Burman

The ways in which discourse research can open up texts, and produce innovative analysis is evident from the preceding chapters, and we have already rehearsed advantages of the approach (Chapter 1, this volume). In this chapter we turn to the disadvantages. Each of the contributors to this book has drawn attention to problems with the methods they adopted, and we will briefly review some of these before going on to outline some of the deeper dangers with the discourse analytic approach. The bulk of the chapter consists of criticisms of discourse analysis: we will outline problems that have been identified in current practice, problems in the framework as a whole, problems that flow from attempts to escape these issues, problems which arise, as a consequence, in teaching the approach and problems attending the wholesale application of the approach to everything. We will conclude with some questions about the way forward for discourse analysis.

FIRST PROBLEMS

The development of a newly arrived approach will meet, as a matter of course, objections from the host discipline, and the drawbacks to discourse analysis identified in the preceding chapters pick up some of the concerns of the mainstream in psychology. Six issues immediately emerge, and some of these will undoubtedly appear in criticisms of discourse analytic studies a researcher may produce.

Six problems of method

The first three problems are ones that will be relevant to most types of research currently carried out in psychology. (i) Discourse analysis is, as Gill (Chapter 6, this volume) points out, very labour-intensive. The task of trawling through pages of interview transcript (not to mention the transcribing of the material in the first place if interviews or recorded discussions are used) is a tedious and time-consuming one. In this respect, discourse analysis, as with many other varieties of qualitative research is usually *more* difficult than positivist number crunching (Banister *et al.*, forthcoming). (ii) It is difficult to determine whether the different repertoires or discourses are present in the text as discrete phenomena, or whether the changes in context are responsible for changes in meaning. As Macnaghten (Chapter 4, this volume) points out, it is sometimes difficult to determine that *different* discourses are at work. Marshall and Raabe (Chapter 3, this volume) are also worried about the idea that we could imagine that we were simply 'letting discourses emerge'. Discourses are not already there waiting to be found but emerge (as much through our work of reading as from the text). (iii) It is difficult to move from a specific text, from a particular usage, to a wider context (Macnaghten, Chapter 4, this volume), and it is frustrating to feel that, as Gill says, we cannot make broad empirical generalizations; there is thus a 'failure to theorize universal processes'. Widdicombe (Chapter 6, this volume) makes the related point that discourse analysts do not give any indication of the frequency of usage of rhetorical devices.

These concerns flowing from the standpoint of traditional psychology can be augmented by three problems that express the frustration of analysts wanting to do critical work, and wanting discourse analysis to be a critical approach. (iv) The analyst is often restricted, for practical reasons (having to fit a research project into a limited space or time), to the confines of the text. It is often the case, as Marshall and Raabe (Chapter 3, this volume) say, that there is often little opportunity for consideration of large-scale political consequences of the repertoires in the material being studied. While this could be seen simply as a problem of reductionism hitting social psychologists again (Billig, 1976), there are particular ironies, and issues to be confronted when the repertoires have been understood as having their source in the surrounding social and political context. (v) The traditional complaint that discourse research does not provide a sufficiently rigorous methodology, in which the reader is satisfied that the analysis has produced the only possible reading, is mirrored in Stenner's (Chapter 7, this volume) complaint – that the analysis tempts us into trying to close the text to alternative readings.

To introduce closure is to do violence to the variety of possible interpretations that could be given of the text when it comes to life in a discourse analytic reading (and to the variety of possible meanings which were present to those who once wrote or spoke the text).

(vi) There is a further problem here which follows from that of bringing about closure, which is to do with the power of the analyst to impose meanings upon another('s) text. Stenner (Chapter 7, this volume) argues that there are ethical problems in having 'power and control over other people's words', and Widdicombe (Chapter 6, this volume) raises the issue of experts legitimating discourse. These are issues of power and morality in research. As part of a movement in research that rejected the dehumanizing methods of traditional psychology, it is right that discourse analysts should consider the power of the researcher as expert, and, as Marks (Chapter 8, this volume) argues, the exercise of power is all the worse when covered over by the illusion of 'democratization' and the disingenuous fantasy of 'empowerment'. Are there more problems that threaten to enmire the researcher? There are.

Six further problems of method

We can supplement the six issues raised by the contributors to this book with a further six identified, in a commentary on discourse analytic research in Britain, by Figueroa and López (1991). These problems appear, at first glance, to be of a different type from those raised so far, for they look as if they could be solved (if the researcher did her research properly). This appearance, however, is deceptive since these are problems of another order that demand critical and challenging reflection on the parameters of the research framework and process. (vii) There is a serious danger of attempting to prevent the analysis of grammatical constructions from leading to an analysis of the social relations implied by discursive forms. Some varieties of discourse analysis (particularly that influenced by post–structuralism) do deliberately focus on social relations and 'subject positions' in discourse, but even here the temptation for the researcher is to simply identify rhetorical devices (or repertoires, or discourses), and the report of the analysis neglects the way that language always does things, always reproduces or transforms social relationships. The analysis threatens to avoid the 'performative' aspect of language (Bowers and Iwi, 1991).

The production of different social relations in different discourses is overdetermined by the production of different social relations in different texts. (viii) Not only are there different social relations set up in different discourses, but different types of text work in different ways (they are accessible to different readers, and are read according to their form and context). There is a risk of taking what one imagines to be the 'method' of discourse analysis and applying it to all texts, without bearing these differences in text in mind. This would become particularly important if the framework was used to analyse texts which were not written or spoken (art, filmic or music texts). The fact that the discourse analytic strand of psychology has tended to focus on spoken or written texts (as reflected within this book) suggests that this is an issue that we are evading rather than resolving. (ix) A related problem here, and a symptom of confusion over competing styles of analysis, is that of using such terms as 'discourse', 'text', 'narrative', 'theme' and 'story' as if they were interchangeable. The meanings and uses of these particular terms need to be carefully specified.

The next three problems concern deeper issues to do with the overarching analytic framework and commitments of the researcher. (x) There is a danger of idealism, not only with reference to the problems of relativism and voluntarism (which we discuss below), but also in the attention only to language at the expense of an attention to the materiality of power. Although power is certainly (re)produced in discourse, power is also at work in the structural position of people when they are not speaking. Power relations endure when the text stops (Parker, 1992a). In part, the reluctance of psychologists to engage with the issue of power in a systematic way is a result of the focus historically of the discipline of psychology upon the individual. Other disciplines are left to deal with societal factors. (xi) There is a serious separate issue here in the isolation of psychology from other disciplines, and the attempt to confine analysis to psychology. This is manifested in the problem of 'competence', the reluctance to address the degree to which the cultural competence of the reader is necessary. Some awareness of cultural trends, of allusions to political and social developments, is essential for a discourse analysis to work. If you do not know what a text is referring to, you cannot produce a reading. (xii) The problem of the (lack of) cultural knowledge of a reader is echoed by another problem which is that of the position of the reader as researcher. Contributors to this book pointed to the problem of power relations between researcher and researched and the ethics of imposing meanings, but in the process of reflection we also have to be aware of the way in which analysts are not only readers but also producers of discourse. They are implicated in the production of the forms of knowledge they describe. To offer a reading of a text is, in some manner or other, to reproduce or transform it.

And another two problems of method: interpretive vigilance and ambivalence

We hesitate to add these further two problems identified by Figueroa and López (1991), for they apply to the contributions in this book, largely as a result of our editorial decisions as to which material should be brought together here. These points, however, should be included, for they pertain to the overall state of discourse analytic research (of which this book is but a symptom). (xiii) There is in several of the chapters collected here a sensitivity to the way language is gendered, but there is still a question as to how what Figueroa and Lopez call the 'interpretive vigilance' exercised by feminists over readings could be extended to include an attention to other varieties of oppression. Despite the panic (particularly in the United States) at present over 'political correctness' in language (Robbins, 1991), we still do believe that a moral/political sensitivity to the way oppression is maintained in language is required of discourse analysts (who are supposed to be aware of social relations in texts). (xiv) An ambivalence (and we use the word advisedly) over the use of psychoanalytic concepts is a problem that we have exhibited in this book. The book chapters collected here contain no explicit discussion of psychoanalysis. This is not so much of a problem because there are forms of discourse analysis appearing which use psychoanalysis (Walkerdine, 1988; Hollway, 1989; Parker, 1992a). Rather, the (more complex) problem here is that discourse analysts are pursuing their texts in a way that is suspicious of what is manifest, and looking to hidden meanings. We use terms, for example, like 'overdetermination' (to refer to the multiple causation of semantic phenomena) and at the same time seem wary of making the connections with psychoanalysis, a 'hermeneutics of suspicion' *par excellence*.

The fourteen problems we have outlined so far have already touched on more fundamental problems than those pertaining to the refinement of technique. Now we want to pursue these deeper issues further. We will organize our reservations about discourse analysis by using the notions of 'empiricism' and 'constructionism', for it appears to us that these terms are not in a type of opposition in which one is right and one is wrong, but are twin problems. The rush to constructionism that discourse analytic research hastens is not a solution to the empiricism of orthodox psychology (an empiricism that discourse analysts wish to escape).

EMPIRICISM AND CONSTRUCTIONISM

Psychology traditionally adopts an 'empiricist' approach to human action. This means not only that the discipline favours empirical work, and would like to check theories against the world (and we would agree that empirical studies are necessary), but rather it means that it adopts the view that the only knowledge worth having (or that it is *possible* to have) is derived from the prediction and control of (probabilistic) laws of behaviour. This refusal to acknowledge the role of theory in the production of knowledge (except when it is viewed as 'bias'), and a fetish with the collection of what it thinks are neutral facts, is empiricism. Harré makes the point that the refusal of empiricists to look deeper than the surface, and the compulsive measurement of what is going on at the surface, is closely connected to an inability to cope with uncertainty: 'The more powerful and speculative, the deeper do our theories purport to go in the exploration of nature, the less can we be certain of their correctness' (Harré, 1981: 9). The only way that psychologists can be certain about things is to cling to what they can measure. Empiricism is bound up with an obsession with truth.

The shift to discourse analysis is ostensibly part of a movement away from empiricism towards social constructionism (Gergen, 1985). Social constructionism encompasses a range of approaches in psychology which share the view that our knowledge about ourselves is culturally bounded, and that different cultural (and subcultural) systems entail different psychologies, sometimes called 'indigenous psychologies' (Heelas and Lock, 1981). The traditional empiricist psychologists are ridiculed for their preoccupation with truth, and constructionism instead looks to a more open analysis of the way 'psychology' changes from culture to culture, from historical period to historical period, and the way our knowledge of that psychology will necessarily also change. There is a profound connection between psychology and culture, and we have to take care not to misunderstand how that connection works and, in particular, in which direction that connection operates. Empiricist psychologists might go so far as to acknowledge that psychological theory seeps out into culture and affects it (and this undoubtedly does happen), but social constructionists (and we would count ourselves among them on this point) would say that it is more the case that culture contains particular distinct types of psychology which seep *into* and mould the discipline of 'psychology'.

It is all the more paradoxical and disturbing, then, to find discourse analysis in practice slipping from social constructionism back to empiricism. We have two suggestions as to why this should be, but we want first to offer examples, describe some of the problems in discourse analysis, that are connected to this slide to empiricism. The set of problems here occurs in the teaching of the approach.

Back to empiricism: a further seven problems

By 'teaching' we mean all attempts to persuade someone that discourse analysis is a 'good thing' and to explain why. One of the worrying aspects of discourse analysis is the abstract character of the debates. The theoretical framework is not easy to understand, and as such it is open to the charge of elitism when we elaborate an analysis which defies simple exposition and which explicitly resists generalized description or easy 'how–to–do–it' rules. What we want to deal with here now is how discourse analysis can function in ways that are compatible with traditional empiricist research through our efforts to make it more accessible.

Reactions of those new to discourse analysis is broadly of two sorts, and their reactions constitute two further problems. (xv) For a first group without a political commitment or framework, the approach is either incomprehensible or irrelevant. The only way to deal with this confusion is for them to learn 'how to do it' and so slip into an alternative, and more dangerous position, in which they treat the analytic style as applicable to the deconstruction of anything and everything. (xvi) In contrast, a discourse framework holds an implicit appeal to a second group, those who already have some political sense and can recognize its relevance and scope. They know already that language contains and reinforces ideology. Those who are already politicized do discourse analysis without knowing that they have done it, or what it is that they have done. They have simply generated the analysis that makes sense to them in a fairly atheoretical, but politically informed, way. Then, to this second group, the relativism ushered in by some aspects of reflexivity is frustrating since it supports the prevailing taboo on politics in the academe. It then becomes a route from politics to opportunism.

These two problems in the reactions of those we teach pale into insignificance when we turn to consider the problems we reproduce when we teach it. We will identify five problems here. (xvii) The first is that of treating it as a value-free technology. The easiest (and safest) way to teach discourse analysis is to present it as a technology, as a theory-free method or as a tool to do research. This encourages the view that discourse analysis can be 'applied', that it is an 'it' (Potter *et al.*, 1990). The project to 'identify' discourses not only sets up a divide between method and interpretation that flies in the face of an emphasis on reflexivity in the new wave of anti-positivist psychology, but through this it also sets up a position of separation between the discourse analyst and the text. In our second-year undergraduate 'discourse analysis' self-directed practicals in Manchester, for example, students are told *not* to be reflexive, because they do a reflexive analysis in their 'interviewing' practical. We collude in the value-free technology game when we support such a bizarre diversion of work. In the activity of determining the scope of, and terms within, discourses we imagine that the boundaries which we are setting are necessary in order to make the work manageable. But in doing this we are also subscribing to a fantasy of non-involvement in the material we are analysing not dissimilar from the traditional methodologies we turned to discourse analysis to escape.

(xviii) We are also ineluctably caught in the trap of reifying the discourse. Further empiricist dangers lurk within discourse analysis's tendency towards abstraction. Depicting discourses as abstract and autonomous meaning systems that float above social practice, or that constitute social practice in mysterious ways, can work to remove discourse analysis from the realms of everyday life. It becomes an academic pursuit, and so we are continually subject to the charge of reifying discourse (Potter *et al.*, 1990). Additional difficulties are involved in specifying the relationship between discourses and the social practices that give rise to them. Just as empiricism constructs its model of the world, treats what it measures as the real (by the process of 'operationalizing' its concepts), so discourse analysis may be in danger of mistaking discourse as the sum total, rather than the manifestation of, structural relationships.

(xix) Although we want to show that discourse research produces more interesting analyses than traditional psychology, we cannot pretend that we are able to 'discover' things in the way that the rest of the discipline thinks it does, and in our attempt to flee from this we encounter the problem of banality. If discourse analysis tends towards overcomplexity and abstraction, it also encounters difficulties in dealing with the familiar. Perhaps we could justify the (imaginary) separation between researcher and text as working to 'defamiliarize', or make strange, everyday practices in which we are ordinarily embedded in order to more clearly investigate their rules and structures. We could see it as a sort of critical-analytic ethnography; discourse analysis tries to elucidate webs of meaning, and the relations and consequences of competing meaning frameworks. But one problem we encounter is that we find it difficult to classify or categorize the seemingly 'obvious'. The analysis can seem like 'common sense', a charge which echoes popular, and well-founded, resistance to mainstream psychology.

(xx) The next problem in teaching is where we encounter once again, in a modified form, the perils of reductionism. In this respect, discourse analysis has clear continuities with empiricism, and this continuity lies in its reductionist tendencies. This reductionism can be either of the psychological or sociological variety, and here the problem appears as one of voluntarism (or, to counter that, crude anti-humanism). The explicit or implicit identification of intentional agents manipulating discourses or engaging in discursive strategies (because there is an inadequately theorized notion of resistance and discursive position) smacks of a voluntarism that tends also towards cognitivism. On the other hand, the conception of discourses as if they were 'tectonic plates' whose clashes constitute subjectivity can present so distributed a notion of power that there is no room for agency, thus also lapsing into mechanistic explanation (Potter *et al.*, 1990). The problem here is macro-reduction to discursive structures which complements micro-reduction to individual agency, giving rise to a different, but equally unhelpful, illusory or limited scope for struggle.

(xxi) Finally, we have to resort too often (in our desire to be clear in our account of how discourse analysis could be done) to atemporality and ahistoricism. The elaboration of a range of positions in relation to language (even when it is seen as social practice) does not necessarily imply a commitment to change those positions. There is a danger that in delineating the structure of (albeit historically constituted) discursive relations we implicitly overemphasize the static features of discursive relations. This is an effect which, paradoxically, threatens to reinstate discourses as being as universal, fixed and timeless. It is necessary for discourse analysis to theorize fluctuations and transformations in discursive relations to ward off a reading of them as unchanging.

From constructionism to empiricism

We suggest that there are two causes of this last cluster of seven problems. The first is to do with the location of this research in traditional academic institutions. Although we argued earlier in the book (Chapter 1) that the existence of discourse groups and discourse units as supportive environments for the development of discourse research and theory is necessary, there is still the question of how the rules of institutions (and the career ambitions and investments of participants who have to work within those rules) deform critical thought, and ensure that radical work plays the game. In many respects, our problems in relaying discourse work to others is a function of that context. The second cause is to do with the nature of contemporary culture, and the transition, in some sectors (particularly some academic sectors) of culture from 'modernity' to 'postmodernity' (Lyotard, 1984; Burman, 1992a; Parker, 1992b). Two important characteristics of the postmodern turn in culture are the shift from depth to surface and the shift from a belief in truth to a celebration of the impossibility of truth, to uncertainty. This double shift, the flight from depth and truth, is, we believe, the cultural setting for discourse analysis. And, in the way that changes in culture always provide the conditions of possibility for changes in (the discipline of) psychology, this setting encourages a variety of discourse analysis which is simultaneously hostile to notions of depth (as empiricism always was) and happy with uncertainty (which empiricism traditionally was not). Discourse analysis, then, risks mutating into a form of postmodern constructionist empiricism.

Empiricism and imperialism: three more problems

The next twist, and it is exacerbated when culture itself increasingly appears to take a postmodern form (that is, it appears to be only surface and to be revelling in uncertainty), is that discourse analysis turns into a form of academic imperialism. This happens when it is used to give sense to all everyday discursive clashes. That everyday clashes of meaning can be informed by discourse analysis is clear. The issue is whether this is always helpful. When is discourse analysis useful, and when is it useless?

These three problems are as follows, and they each revolve around the slogan 'you don't have to be a discourse analyst to see that . . .'. (xxii) The first concerns the question as to whether discourse research is taken to be applicable to an issue because it is 'interesting', or whether it should be applicable because the issue is embedded in a particular and significant context. Is discourse analysis the goal, or should we rather be using it strategically (with other goals in mind). For example, the claim by some male lecturers that there is no moral problem in sleeping with students is often justified by an appeal to the liberal notion of 'choice'. The student in higher education is an adult, so the claim goes, and so it is up to her to 'choose'. That this position obscures (excuses, and abuses) power is a point that a discourse analyst could easily miss. An analysis of the connections between notions of choice used here and free-market images of choice used to justify inequality in economic relationships (between owner and worker, producer and consumer) might be seen merely as 'interesting', and it would skirt the real issue. The notion of 'choice' is used here rhetorically to hide power, and you don't have to be a discourse analyst to see that.

(xxiii) A second, related, issue is whose analysis we are dealing with. This sets up further questions of practice in terms of the positions the discourse analyst constructs. The current plans for 'community treatment' of people who have experienced mental distress are interpreted by self-advocacy groups as thinly disguised devices for their regulation and control (e.g. BNAP, 1988; Lawson, 1988; LAMHA, 1988). Here, the analysis offered by the group we would presumably want to support coincides with that offered by post-structuralists (e.g. Foucault, 1975). However, in this case, the job of the progressive discourse analyst is surely to publicize the analyses presented by these groups rather than expropriate them, rather than presenting them as if they were *ours*. To unravel the rhetorical tricks of those in power is part of politics, and you don't have to be a discourse analyst to do that.

(xxiv) The next problem is to do with normalization, and normalizing powers, of the discipline. Clearly, the rise of a particular approach within the academe is overdetermined, but there are certain dilemmas, not to mention dangers of ahistoricism at work here. There is something colonizing about the current vogue for discourse analysis which invites people retrospectively to recast what they have done as 'discourse analysis' or persuades us to 'recognize' them as 'really' being discourse analysts. The drive to constitute a specific method or area called 'discourse analysis' can be seen as arising from the pressures of academic practice. This stems from the need to 'discover' new approaches, get jobs and establish corporate identities (such as 'discourse units') within a market-oriented academic landscape. There are many powerful studies of language around, and you don't have to be a discourse analyst to take them seriously.

In this last cluster of three problems, the connection with politics is clearly at issue. Now we want to turn explicitly to the politics of discourse analysis.

DISCOURSE AND POLITICS

Is the progressive moral/political impulse associated with discourse work a necessary or intrinsic feature of the approach? This is a vital question for researchers who turn to discourse analytic research because it seems to offer a critical framework, not only for understanding accounts (the 'data') but also for understanding why the rest of psychology cannot deal with textual material. It is important to address this question in order to counter the general reformist and recuperative dynamic of academic practice (that is, the way the academic world absorbs criticisms and makes them a part of itself and all the stronger as a result). Given the undoubtedly helpful work conducted within the framework of discourse analysis, as the preceding chapters indicate, it is tempting to see this critical dynamic as somehow inherent within the approach itself, rather than as simply a feature of the way it is used. We need to take care to distinguish between the radical or politicizing 'applications' of discourse analysis and any radical claims made for the theory itself. It does sometimes seem that such politics as do underlie varieties of discourse approaches are either ambiguous or even, occasionally, hostile to critical work. We will identify four problems here, and then four traps (additional corresponding problems) that occur when a researcher tries to escape these problems. (Boardgame to follow!)

Four political problems

(xxv) The first is the problem of relativism. Acknowledging readings as multiple and mutually co-existent can work to usefully problematize and disrupt dominant accounts. Meanings are tied to the time and space in which they are elaborated. Hence claims to universal timeless truths made by social sciences such as psychology are thrown into question. This is fine when we want to criticize or disrupt accounts by indicating how there is no fixed interpretation. We may do this when we want to challenge the truth claims of dominant psychological models for example. However, it becomes difficult, using this model, to elaborate a position where it is possible to privilege or maintain a commitment to one reading rather than another (Burman, 1992b). In other words, a motivated, partisan political orientation is proscribed. Theory floats disconnected from any political position, and this is a return to a disturbingly familiar liberal pluralist position.

(xxvi) The problem of difference is connected to that of liberal pluralism in discourse analysis. The attention to variability, and then to difference within the discourse framework which initially seemed so fruitful and sympathetic to feminist concerns, for example, has proved to be limited in practice. There is a necessary conceptual link between notions of 'variability' in language and of 'difference' in meaning. The emphasis on the specificity of situations, and of sociohistorical conditions tends towards a fragmentation of positions, making collective action difficult. Such collective action would necessarily be 'unitary' (bring things together as one type of force or 'collective subject'), and would sit uncomfortably with discourse analysis's critique of the rational integrated subject (Eagleton, 1991).

(xxvii) The attention to difference then brings in its wake the 'problem' of resistance, or of making resistance problematic. The notion of discursive position has been a fruitful area for the politicized use of discourse analysis. Analysts have shown how it is possible to use multiple positionings within discourse to negotiate power relations (Hudson, 1984; Walkerdine, 1981). Yet where difference reigns supreme, so resistance threatens to be envisaged primarily only as residing within the individual. Although of all the theorists contributing to the discourse 'package', Foucault (1980, 1981) has the most developed and explicit analysis of power, this is still located within individual and spontaneous reactions (capillaries of micro-power resisted by the body), rather than planned, directed struggle. Power is seen as so distributed within the mutual and changing relations of institutions as to remain an intangible and inescapable condition of subjectivity. The analysis of power as all-pervasive threatens to usher in an exhausted and passive fatalism and surrender of political vision. If power is everywhere, and where there is power there is resistance, then why bother trying to change the order of things?

(xxviii) The issue of reflexivity becomes a problem when it becomes part of the solution. Reflexivity has been useful in exploring researcher involvement and effects. However, focusing on the researcher's construction of the account rather than what is being accounted for has its problems too. Here, the key question concerns the status of the account. This issue crops up in the form of worries about how everything is being reduced to discourse, for how can we interpret anything if all meanings relate only to each other and not to something outside? Self-referentiality breeds solipsism. We agree with those who wish to focus on signification, language as productive when it has no 'referents' outside (Henriques *et al.*, 1984), but it is also important to hold onto some notion of representation. Representation and interpretation presuppose the independent existence of that which is represented or interpreted, but a strong discourse position tries to deny this. First, the emphasis can shift the focus to the account rather than what is being accounted for. Second, wallowing in the researcher's interpretive assumptions and processes can detract from the importance of the topic and possible political interventions. Third, agonizing about subjectivity and power can lead worried researchers to abandon the project of making interventions that go beyond reflexive concerns because of anxieties about exploitation or the paternalist relations set up in research.

Attempts to escape the problems: four more problems

In the attempts of researchers to grapple with the four problems we have just identified, there is a danger that the attention to subjectivity could work in four equally deleterious ways. (xxix) It can work to treat interpretive processes as matters to be confessed as interfering with the account (as when the research is said to be merely 'subjective'). (xxx) It can work to constitute the account (as when the research is offered as one person's valid opinion of what is happening). (xxxi) The subjectivity of interpretation could be seen as detaching the analysis from reality, rather than explicitly positioning the researcher within the research (as when the research is claimed to be 'just' an account). (xxxii) If all research is rendered only fictive, then it can be said that we cannot make material interventions with our work, because our work is just another fiction. (This arises when the researcher claims that she had 'no effects' on her interviewees). Taking these problems together, we start to glimpse the vista of interpretive regress, and political immobilization, that could lie ahead for overenthusiastic discourse analysts.

What this review of political problems with discourse analysis suggests is that it does not offer a political position in its own right: The politics can only lie in the strategic appropriation of the framework.

This, indeed, is the position that is developing amongst feminists who have been using discourse work (in its broadest sense) outside psychology. Discourse frameworks were taken up by feminists in particular as providing a welcome relief from single-factor models of oppression which deny or devalue varieties of struggle. However, the reception of discourse analysis by feminists has shifted from an initial enthusiasm (e.g. Weedon, 1987) to increasing caution emerging from across a spectrum of disciplines as diverse as philosophy (Lovibond, 1989), geography (Bondi, 1990), film theory (Creed, 1987; Penley, 1989) and cultural studies (Moore, 1988).

CONCLUSIONS AND DIRECTIONS

This survey of thirty-two problems with discourse analytic research is not exhaustive. There may be fifty-seven varieties of problem! Some points we have noted here have been developed at greater length elsewhere (Burman, 1991), and there have been other criticisms of discourse analysis outlined by different writers (Bowers, 1988; Abrams and Hogg, 1990). The problems we have identified have, in some cases, been problems to do with the turn to language in psychology, particularly in its post-structuralist forms (Burman, 1990).

Discourse analysis will undoubtedly develop in ways which will 'solve' some of the problems, and make others worse. Directions that the approach is moving in, or could move in, have been identified at meetings of discourse researchers. Figueroa and López (1991) noted five striking 'absences' in their encounter with discourse analysis in Britain, absences which we can here note also as suggestions for issues that discourse analysis could turn to address. Each absence also signifies something important about the state and future of discourse analysis: (i) The methodological process by which the material was produced (masked by an implicit intuitivism in some cases); (ii) discussion of the institutional appropriation of the 'method' as part of the apparatus of traditional psychology; (iii) the relation between discourse and modes of production, not only in texts studied but in the approach (why this approach now?); (iv) the link between the rise of discourse analysis and the contemporary 'crisis of knowledge' (postmodernity and the suchlike); and (v) how the analysis of discourse is related to the cultural space which is its context (for example, in the ideological and political forms of British society).

These absences, and perhaps we could take them now alongside the thirty-two problems, raise all the traditional questions of models and morals of research in psychology, and more. The positions outlined in the chapters in this book do offer visions for making worthwhile political interventions using discourse analysis. This activity may take a variety of forms. Discourse analysts now can champion the cause of a particular discourse by elaborating the contrasting consequences of each discursive framework, and can promote an existing (perhaps subordinate) discourse (as the 'empowerment', 'giving people a voice' model of research). We can intervene directly in clarifying consequences of discursive frameworks with speakers (as in training or action research, for example), as well as commenting on the discursive–political consequences of discursive clashes and frameworks. If we do not do one or all of these, we will be assimilated into mainstream empiricist research. We would then find our work relayed among the repertoires of the discipline, rather than offering, as it should, critical readings of its texts.

REFERENCES

Abrams, D. and Hogg, M. (1990) 'The context of discourse: let's not throw out the baby with the bathwater', *Philosophical Psychology* 3 (2): 219–25.

Banister, P., Burman, E., Parker, I., Taylor, M. and Tindall, C. (forthcoming) *Qualitative Methods in Psychology: A Research Guide*, Milton Keynes: Open University Press.

Billig, M. (1976) *Social Psychology and Intergroup Relations*, London: Academic Press.

BNAP (British Network for Alternatives to Psychiatry) (1988) 'Community Treatment Orders 2: Letter to Mental Health Commission', *Asylum: a Magazine for Democratic Psychiatry* 12 (3): 4–5.

Bondi, L. (1990) 'Feminism, postmodernism and geography: space for women? Feminism and postmodernism', *Antipode* 22 (2): 156–67.

Bowers, J. (1988) 'Essay review of *Discourse and Social Psychology*', *British Journal of Social Psychology* 27: 185–92.

Bowers, J. and Iwi, K. (1991) 'Constructing society: beyond discursive idealism and social constructionism', paper for Second Discourse Analysis Workshop/Conference, Manchester Polytechnic, July.

Burman, E. (1990) 'Differing with deconstruction: a feminist critique', in I. Parker and J. Shotter (eds) *Deconstructing Social Psychology*, London: Routledge.

—— (1991) 'What discourse is not', *Philosophical Psychology* 4 (3): 325–42.

—— (1992a) 'Developmental psychology and the postmodern child', in J. Doherty, E. Graham and M. Malek (eds) *Postmodernism and the Social Sciences*, London: Macmillan.

—— (1992b) 'Feminism and discourse in developmental psychology: power, subjectivity and interpretation', *Feminism & Psychology* 2 (1): 45–59.

Creed, B. (1987) 'From here to modernity: feminism and postmodernism', *Postmodern Screen* 2: 47–67.

Eagleton, T. (1991) *Ideology: An Introduction*, London: Verso.

Figueroa, H. and López, M. (1991) 'Commentary on Discourse Analysis Workshop/Conference', paper for Second Discourse Analysis Workshop/Conference, Manchester Polytechnic, July.

Foucault, M. (1975) *The Birth of the Clinic*, New York: Random House.

—— (1980) *Power/Knowledge: Selected Interviews and Other Writings 1972-1977*, Hassocks, Sussex: Harvester Press.

—— (1981) *The History of Sexuality: Volume 1: An Introduction*, Harmondsworth: Pelican.

Gergen, K.J. (1985) 'The social constructionist movement in modern psychology', *American Psychologist* 40: 266–75.

Harré, R. (1981) 'The positivist–empiricist approach and its alternative', in P. Reason and J. Rowan (eds) *Human Inquiry: A Sourcebook of New Paradigm Research*, Chichester: Wiley.

Heelas, P. and Lock, A. (eds) (1981) *Indigenous Psychologies: The Anthropology of the Self*, London: Academic Press.

Henriques, J. Hollway, W., Urwin, C., Venn, C. and Walkerdine, V. (1984) *Changing the Subject: Psychology, Social Regulation and Subjectivity*, London: Methuen.

Hollway, W. (1989) *Subjectivity and Method in Psychology: Gender, Meaning and Science*, London: Sage.

Hudson, B., (1984) 'Femininity and adolescence', in A. McRobbie and M. Nava (eds) *Gender and Generation*, Basingstoke: Macmillan.

LAMHA (London Alliance for Mental Health Action) (1988) 'Community Treatment Orders 3: Statement', *Asylum: A Magazine for Democratic Psychiatry* 12 (3): 5–7.

Lawson, D. (1988) 'Community Treatment Orders 1: the problem', *Asylum: A Magazine for Democratic Psychiatry* 12 (3): 3–4.

Lovibond, S. (1989) 'Feminism and postmodernism', *New Left Review* 178: 5–28.

Lyotard, J. (1984) *The Postmodern Condition: a Report on Knowledge*, Manchester: Manchester University Press.

Moore, S. (1988) 'Getting a bit of the other: the pimps of postmodernism', in R. Chapman and J. Rutherford (eds) *Male Order: Unwrapping Masculinity*, London: Lawrence & Wishart.

Parker, I. (1992a) *Discourse Dynamics: Critical Analysis for Social and Individual Psychology*, London: Routledge.
—— (1992b) 'Discourse discourse: social psychology and postmodernity', in J. Doherty, E. Graham and M. Malek (eds) *Postmodernism and the Social Sciences*, London: Macmillan.
Penley, C. (1989) '"A certain refusal of difference": feminism and film theory', in *The Future of an Illusion*, London: Routledge.
Potter, J., Wetherell, M., Gill, R. and Edwards, D. (1990) 'Discourse – noun, verb or social practice', *Philosophical Psychology* 3 (2): 205–17.
Robbins, B. (1991) 'Tenured radicals, the new McCarthyism and "PC"', *New Left Review* 188: 151–7.
Walkerdine, V. (1981) 'Sex, power and pedagogy', *Screen Education* 38: 14–21.
—— (1988) *The Mastery of Reason: Cognitive Development and the Production of Rationality*, London: Routledge.
Weedon, C. (1987) *Post-structuralist Theory and Feminist Practice*, Oxford: Blackwell.

Name index

Subject index